LIVE YOUR BEST LIFE NOW! 4/5/19

Stephen F. Brown

STEPHEN F. BROWN

LIVE YOUR BEST LIFE NOW

By Stephen F. Brown

A Publication of:
Stephen F. Brown
Abundant Life Faith Fellowship Church
2740 Hyannis Drive
Cincinnati, Ohio 45251

Website www.alff.org

Email: thealff@alff.org

ISBN-13: 978-1533081636

ISBN-10: 1533081638

Published by:
New Vision Publishing Services
Cincinnati, Ohio - USA

newvisionbookspublishers@gmail.com

www.newvisionpublishers.com

TABLE OF CONTENTS

About the Author

Elder Stephen F. Brown is a native of Cincinnati, Ohio. He was saved in April of 1972 and filled with the Holy Spirit at Zion Temple First Pentecostal Church. He presently serves as the Senior Elder of Abundant Life Faith Fellowship Church located in Colerain Township. Abundant Life is a nondenominational church which he and his wife Marion founded in their family room in April of 1981. His heart is to build character and spiritual maturity in those called to be followers of Christ so they can live a winning and victorious Christian life.

Elder Steve teaches and proclaims the truths of the uncompromising Word of God with integrity, fervor and sound character. He operates in the ministry offices of a Pastor and Teacher with the manifestations of the gifts of the Spirit in operation. He has traveled to several countries in Africa and India where he shared the Good News of Jesus Christ.

He is also the author of the book, *The Parable of The Sower*, which is a perfect example of his explicit teaching. He and Marion are the parents of four adult children and twelve grandchildren.

ACKNOWLEDGMENTS

I dedicate this book to my wife Marion, our four children, Darren, Lamont, Charnee', Tammy and our twelve grandchildren.

I also want to acknowledge my church family here at Abundant Life Faith Fellowship (ALFF). Without their help this book would not be possible.

I am thankful for the teachers, preachers and other people who have crossed my path and influenced my thinking over the last forty plus years.

Lastly, I thank God for my brothers and sisters in Kenya, who were inspirational in me writing this book.

Love,
Stephen F. Brown

Foreword

I have known Pastor Stephen Brown as a man with a compassionate heart to help people. God has blessed him with exceptional wisdom and insight in teaching biblical principles that apply to everyday life issues. I have been privileged to glean from his wealth of wisdom on organization, team leadership, financial stewardship, investment and much more. Many lives have been empowered and changed through his teaching ministry.

I feel honored to recommend to you his new book, Live Your Best Life Now, which is a treasure trove of practical principles of living a better life. This book highlights the abundant life that Jesus promised in John 10:10 AMP, *I came that they may have and enjoy life, and have it in abundance [to the full, till it overflows]*. Pastor Brown explains that true happiness and fulfillment in life is only found in God and when we pursue His plan and purpose for our lives, we will experience the fullness of life.

Many people want a better life but they do not believe it is possible given the circumstances and situations they may be facing. This book will challenge you to change your mindset so that you may see all the positive possibilities you can achieve in your life when you step out to be all that God has called you to be. God has so many promises for us that we do not tap into. Get ready to be taught, equipped and empowered with profound wisdom and knowledge that will set you on the pathway of living your best life now.

Boniface G. Gitau
Author & Publisher
www.newvisionpublishers.com

Chapter One

PUT GOD
FIRST

We are living in a day and time of increasing prices and economic pressures which seem to have no end. Prices keep going up. Manufactures have made many items we buy in the grocery store smaller rather than raising the prices. In reality they have raised the price, but hope you and I don't notice. Gas prices have been going up and down like a roller coaster ride. Many find themselves in economic prisons, not of their making, without a "get out of jail free" card. With economic pressures like this, it's hard for the average person to maintain the bare necessities of life like food, clothing, and keeping a roof over their head.

There seems to be no signs of relief in the near future. Some of you reading this book are not sure how you are going to make ends meet. For those who don't know God, the days ahead are indeed dark days and something to be feared. But for those of us who know God, it should be a different story since we have a different outlook. David said, *"I once was young, but now I am old. But I have never seen the righteous forsaken or his seed begging bread."* As children of God, we should expect to be blessed and to walk in God's divine favor in every area of life.

- **If you want to live your best life now, you must be willing to put God first.**
  When you put God first, you have the right to expect God's favor to hunt you down and insist on being a part of your life. When we put God first, everything else we need in life will be added to us.

Matthew 6:33 (KJV) *But seek ye first the kingdom of God, and his righteousness; and all these things shall be added unto you.*

The Bible teaches us if we love the Lord our God with all our heart, and with all our mind, and all our strength, we will be blessed and

God will put a hedge of protection around us. And that is exactly what God did for Job.

Job 1:10 (KJV) *Hast not thou made an hedge about him, and about his house, and about all that he hath on every side? thou hast blessed the work of his hands, and his substance is increased in the land.*

God put a hedge of protection around Job because Job loved God and was willing to put Him first above all things.

* **Let's take a look at four reasons God put a hedge of protection around Job.**
  Job 1:1 (KJV) *There was a man in the land of Uz, whose name was Job; and that man (1) was perfect (2) and upright, (3) and one that feared God, (4) and eschewed evil.*

If you want to live your best life now, you must be willing to do the same four things Job did. The Bible says God is not a respecter of persons, if He did it for Job, He will do it for you. If you do the same four things Job did, expect to experience God's favor and not be pulled under by the pressures and turmoil of everyday life.

Putting God first is a decision which will cause God to advance you ahead of the line when others say no way when you least expect it.

* **If you want to live your best life now, you must include God first in your plans and follow God's plan for your life.**
  Proverbs 19:21 (NCV) *People can make all kinds of plans, but only the LORD'S plan will happen.*

Proverbs 16:3 (NIV) *Commit to the LORD whatever you do, and your plans will succeed.*

Include God in your plans and watch Him work on your behalf. In order to fulfill your God-given destiny, you must make your plans according to God's purposes and stay focused on fulfilling them. Don't allow yourself to get distracted or side-tracked, spending your time and energy on things that are not God's best for your life. There are many good causes in life.

There are a lot of good things we can spend our time focusing on that are not God's best for us. Someone once said the word good has one more **o** than **God**. Good causes can rob you of God's best for your life.

If you want to live your best life now, you must be willing to put God first.

Remember, God's plans are blessed, and as you walk in them you will experience His abundance in everything you set your hand to do! **James 1:22** says *be doers of the word and not hearers only.* You and I have a part to play in attracting God's blessings to us. If you want to be blessed, you must learn how to hear and do what God and other people that God has placed in your life to help you have to say. Sometimes God will speak to you directly, but there are other times He will speak to you through others He has placed in your life to guide you.

Proverbs 15:22 (MSG) *Refuse good advice and watch your plans fail; take good counsel and watch them succeed.*

- **If you want to live your best life now, you must allow yourself to be led by the Spirit.**
  Romans 8:14 (ESV) *For all who are led by the Spirit of God are sons of God.*

Did you know that you make over 2,500 - 5,000 decisions every day? The quality of your life is determined by the quality of your decisions. Choosing to live according to the Spirit is the most important decision you can make when it comes to living a winning and victorious Christian life. One way God speaks to us is through the Holy Spirit.

John 16:13 (ESV) *When the Spirit of truth comes, he will guide you into all the truth, for he will not speak on his own authority, but whatever he hears he will speak, and he will declare to you the things that are to come.*

> *If you want to live your best life now, you must include God first in your plans and follow God's plan for your life.*

The Holy Spirit is like a GPS guidance system in a car or smart phone. When the Holy Spirit speaks to you, it can seem like a steady drop of rain dripping on the same spot again and again in your mind. When the Holy Spirit speaks to us, many times it feels like a constant impression on the inside that won't leave you alone. Whatever you do, you can't seem to shake it. You can't run fast enough or jump high enough to escape the forcefulness of His presence. God has given us His Spirit to help us make right decisions in every area of life. God has given each of us the ability to choose good and refuse evil. It's called the freedom of choice.

In **Psalm 119:30 (KJV)** David said, "*I have chosen the way of truth*". God has given us the ability to choose the path of truth just as He gave David.

When you refuse to allow yourself to be led by the Holy Spirit, you open the door to a guilty conscience. A guilty conscience will hinder your ability to communicate with God and release your faith. That's why it's so important to stay true to your conscience and quickly repent if you fall into sin. God has great plans in store for you and when you choose to follow His leading, He will guide you on a path of victory in every area of your life! God has laid out a safe path for us to follow that is filled with His blessings if we will only hear Him and obey!

Psalm 37:23 (KJV) *The steps of a good man are ordered by the LORD: and he delighteth in his way.*

Look at yourself in the mirror and say: "You are born to live a life of victory!"

Living a Spirit led life is living a balanced life.

- **If you want to live your best life now, you must wait for God's Plan to unfold. Learning how to wait on God for direction is the key to a safe passage in every area of life.**
  Isaiah 40:31 (AMP) *Those who wait for the Lord, who expect, look for, and hope in Him, shall renew their strength.*

Everything in life won't come your way like ripe cherries falling off a tree. But if you are patient and wait upon the Lord, they will come and good things will happen.

Habakkuk 2:3 (TLB) *But these things I plan won't happen right away. Slowly, steadily, surely, the time approaches when the vision will be fulfilled. If it seems slow, do not despair, for these things will surely come to pass. Just be patient! They will not be overdue a single day!*

I know God has put dreams and desires in your heart; you have things you are hoping for, praying about, and believing God will cause to happen. The Bible says if we'll pray in faith according to

God's Word, God will hear us and answer these prayers. When you have a dream from God in your heart, you don't have to struggle and try to force it to happen. No good will come from beating your head against the walls of life, trying to make God do something.

You don't have to be worried or frustrated wondering if it is ever going to come to pass. When you have the promises of God deep in your heart, the Bible says you will enter into God's rest and in due season or at God's appointed time it will come to pass.

Psalm 1:1-3 (AMP) *BLESSED (HAPPY, fortunate, prosperous, and enviable) is the man who walks and lives not in the counsel of the ungodly [following their advice, their plans and purposes], nor stands [submissive and inactive] in the path where sinners walk, nor sits down [to relax and rest] where the scornful [and the mockers] gather. ² But his delight and desire are in the law of the Lord, and on His law (the precepts, the instructions, the teachings of God) he habitually meditates (ponders and studies) by day and by night. ³ And he shall be like a tree firmly planted [and tended] by the streams of water, ready to bring forth its fruit in its season; its leaf also shall not fade or wither; and everything he does shall prosper [and come to maturity].*

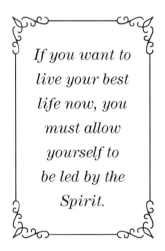

If you want to live your best life now, you must allow yourself to be led by the Spirit.

Waiting for the promises of God to open up in your life is a place of total trust.

Proverbs 3:5-6 (KJV) *Trust in the LORD with all thine heart;*

and lean not unto thine own understanding. [6] *In all thy ways acknowledge him, and he shall direct thy paths.*

One thing I love about this verse of Scripture is the word paths is plural and not singular. In other words, God will direct your path not only once but again and again.

Trusting God is a place where you know beyond a shadow of a doubt that God is going to see you through. When you place your life in God's hands, you can live in a place of peace. If you don't, your life will be void of God's peace and filled with frustrations.

Philippians 4:7 (KJV) *And the peace of God, which passeth all understanding, shall keep your hearts and minds through Christ Jesus.*

Living at peace with God is a place of faith, knowing God will cause your prayers to become a reality. God is always in complete control, and at exactly the right time, He will bring your dream to pass.

Chapter Summary

If you want to live your best life now, it begins by asking Jesus Christ into your heart.

Romans 10:9 (KJV) *That if thou shalt confess with thy mouth the Lord Jesus, and shalt believe in thine heart that God hath raised him from the dead, thou shalt be saved.*

Chapter Two

THE SEARCH
FOR TRUE
HAPPINESS

Proverbs 10:28 (NCV) - *A good person can look forward to happiness, but an evil person can expect nothing.*

The search for happiness has puzzled humankind for thousands of years. People throughout history have tried all kinds of things to find happiness but have repeatedly failed again and again. Is the success, victory, and happiness you desire eluding you like a mysterious fog and slipping through your fingertips every time you reach for them? Do you desire a life with more purpose and meaning? Do you want to be a man or woman that is highly favored by God as were Abraham, Noah or Jesus? True happiness begins with finding God. It all starts with God. If you want to live your best life now, you must start with Jesus.

Col. 1:16 (MSG) - *For everything, absolutely everything, above and below, visible and invisible, rank after rank after rank of angels—everything got started in him and finds its purpose in him.*

You were made by God and for God; and until you understand that, you will never find the happiness you are looking for. Why are some people succeeding in life while others are not? Why do the pieces of the puzzle of life fall in place so easily for some and not for others?

If you want to be happier, successful, and fulfilled in life, say to yourself, "That's me!" Tons of literature have been written on the subject of success over the years, but few people have obtained it, most people are still searching for it as if it were a hidden treasure.

Many scratch their heads in an effort to understand how success works and how to attract it into their lives. What are others doing that causes them to enter into the winner's circle again and again while others are not invited? It should be obvious to us by now that some people are doing something right and others are not. What are some doing right that others are not? The decisions we make in everyday life are the key. I want you to ask yourself the question, what can I do to become more successful? What can I do to excel and succeed in life more than I am right now, whether spiritually, professionally, or personally?

If you want to live your best life now, you must be willing to make a lifelong decision to make wiser decisions by applying the principles and truths of God's Word in your everyday life and never stop learning. I have come to the conclusion that learning and applying the principles of God's Word to our lives is essential and necessary in living a winning and victorious Christian life. Solomon learned this truth many years before you and I were born.

> *If you want to live your best life now, you must be willing to make a lifelong decision to make wiser decisions by applying the principles and truths of God's Word in your everyday life and never stop learning.*

Ecclesiastes 12:13 (CEV) *Everything you were taught can be put into a few words: Respect and obey God! This is what life is all about.*

Sometimes we can't receive God's truth because we are not ready and we have our hands over our ears. I appreciate the saying; *When the student is ready, the teacher will appear.* It's not that the teachers are not teaching the glorious truths of God's Word because they are! In many cases the students just aren't ready to listen. If we fail to learn, we fail to grow, and if we fail to grow we will die spiritually; we will remain spiritual infants and immature followers of Christ. Life gives us endless opportunities to learn, and the more difficult the situation, the more we are likely to learn. Every situation in life can be a teacher in one way or another. We can either learn what to do or what not to do.

> *Every situation in life can be a teacher in one way or another. We can either learn what to do or what not to do.*

Each of us can learn from others, especially the difficult ones – they are like angels sent from heaven to teach us about ourselves. All of life is teaching us something. We learn from everything that happens in the world around us. We learn when things go our way, and we learn when they don't. Most of all, we learn by watching ourselves and observing how we react to the different circumstances in life. We also learn by reflecting deeply on what moves us, how we feel, what we say and what we do.

If you make the following action steps habits to live by, they will lead you to success and victories beyond your wildest dreams. They are not a quick fix or instant cure, but they will help you take a giant step forward in living your best life now!

- **True happiness begins with you being happy with yourself.**
  God made us who we are, and always remember God doesn't make any junk!

Eph. 2:10 (NCV) *God has made us what we are. In Christ*

Jesus, God made us to do good works, which God planned in advance for us to live our lives doing.

You are God's special handiwork, equipped and anointed to be the person God called you to be! The Bible says in Psalm 139 that God knew you before you were ever formed in your mother's womb. You have unique gifts, abilities, and talents, and God has a unique plan for your life. Don't let others try to make you something God never intended for you to be. Don't let anyone make you what they think you ought to be, but seek to be who God created you to be. Learn how to be content in the person God made you to be. Nothing more; nothing less!

Philippians 4:11 (NASB) *Not that I speak from want, for I have learned to be content in whatever circumstances I am.*

Chapter Summary

Resist outside demands and pressures that try to mold you into something else.

Chapter Three

IT'S OK TO DREAM

D
o you often dream of living a more rewarding life? Do you aspire to have a better job, a stronger marriage, a happier home? Do you wish for more gratifying relationships with your family and friends? Perhaps you simply want to accomplish more and leave a lasting legacy for future generations? If you are like most people you have written these things down on your tomorrow's To Do List. You can't pursue what's really important in life because you're too busy with other people's priorities and the mundane responsibilities of everyday life and trying to make a living. How do you break out of this routine and experience the full potential God has for your life? This is where my book, *Living Your Best Life Now* comes in.

The world in which we live tends to focus on the negative rather than the positive. Most people talk more about negative things than positive ones. I would like to turn the table on that kind of thinking and get you to focus on what you say positive rather than negative. As you read through this book, I want you to focus on thinking positive thoughts. I want you to focus your thoughts on what God wants to do for you even if it seems impossible. Dare to believe God for a positive outcome in life rather than the negative ones. The Bible teaches us to think positive thoughts.

Philip. 4:8b (NLT) *Fix your thoughts on what is true and honorable and right. Think about things that are pure and lovely and admirable. Think about things that are excellent and worthy of praise.*

Don't allow the devil to steal your God-given right to live a winning and victorious Christian life now. You don't have to wait until next week, next month or next year, you can experience God's blessings right now!

John 10:10 (MSG) *A thief is only there to steal and kill and*

31

destroy. I came so they can have real and eternal life, more and better life than they ever dreamed of.

Do you want to experience the abundant life Jesus promised you in John 10:10? The Bible tells us as a man thinks or believes in his heart, so is he. How you think about things plays a major role in shaping your reality, and your world around you. Your thoughts are like a taxicab which takes you where you want to go in life. All you have to do is keep it gassed up and keep the meter running. How you think determines what you believe and what you believe determines where you go in life.

> *How you think determines what you believe and what you believe determines where you go in life.*

How you think determines if you can be fully used by God or not. If you believe in your heart you are an overcomer in Christ, you will act like an overcomer, and if you act like an overcomer you will become an overcomer. Whether you realize it or not, your belief system has a huge influence on the outcome of your life.

If you have asked Jesus Christ to come into your heart, you have an unlimited reservoir of God's power and strength residing in you waiting to be tapped and let out. It is yours for the taking.

Ephesians 3:20 (KJV) *Now unto him that is able to do exceeding abundantly above all that we ask or think, according to the power that worketh in us.*

The Message Translation says it this way: *God can do anything, you know—far more than you could ever imagine* *or guess or request in your wildest dreams! He does it not by pushing us around but by working within us, his Spirit deeply and gently within us.*

In **1 John 4:4 (KJV)** it says: *Ye are of God, little children, and have overcome them: because greater is he that is in you, than he that is in the world.*

If you want to live your best life now you must learn how to operate with the faith it takes. When you do, the promises of God will become a living reality in your life. You won't have to look for them, they will look for you. There's something powerful about having faith-filled thoughts and speaking faith-filled words. When your thoughts and your words are filled with victory, your actions and experiences will be filled with victory. Faith-filled thoughts and faith-filled words will fill your heart with courage even in the midst of dark, dangerous and uncertain circumstances that life may bring your way.

> *If you want to live your best life now you must learn how to operate with the faith it takes. When you do, the promises of God will become a living reality in your life.*

- **If you want to live your best life now, you must be fearless and courageous in all that you do.**
  John Wayne said, *"Courage is being scared to death but saddling up any way."*

Your God has promised to lead you into victory in every area of your life.

Chapter Summary

Dare to believe God will do what He said He will do.

II Cor. 2:14 (MSG) *But I thank God, who always leads us in victory because of Christ. Wherever we go, God uses us to make clear what it means to know Christ. It's like a fragrance that fills the air.*

Chapter Four

FAITH FOOD FOR EVERYDAY LIVING

Matthew 4:4 (KJV) *But he answered and said, It is written, Man shall not live by bread alone, but by every word that proceedeth out of the mouth of God.*

Matthew 4:4b (The Message Bible) *It takes more than bread to stay alive. It takes a steady stream of words from God's mouth.*

Faith is the key to bringing the blessings of heaven down to earth now.

Job 23:12 (KJV) *Neither have I gone back from the commandment of his lips; I have esteemed the words of his mouth more than my necessary food.*

Filling your belly with faith food will give you the spiritual strength you need to live day by day.

Eating God's Word will cause faith to come and knock on the door of your spiritual house and say, "May I come in?" Faith comes by hearing and feeding on God's Word.

You must feed yourself God's Word on a daily basis if you want to become a spiritually strong, unstoppable follower of Christ.

Romans 10:17 (KJV) *So then faith cometh by hearing, and hearing by the word of God.*

Once we receive faith, faith must become a way of living.

Habakkuk 2:4b (KJV) *the just shall live by his faith.*

You must feed yourself God's Word on a daily basis if you want to become a spiritually strong, unstoppable follower of Christ. Just as we have to eat natural food daily to keep our bodies healthy and strong, you must eat spiritual food on a daily basis to stay spiritually strong.

- **If you want to live your best life now, you must feed yourself faith food.**

Chapter Summary

Faith comes by reading and hearing God's Word. As we read and hear God's Word we become more informed about what God wants to do in our life.

- **Faith is trusting and believing God will do what He said He would do!**
  Psalm 20:7 (CEV) *Some people trust the power of chariots or horses, but we trust you, LORD God.*

Proverbs 3:5-6 (MSG) *Trust GOD from the bottom of your heart; don't try to figure out everything on your own. [6] Listen for GOD's voice in everything you do, everywhere you go; he's the one who will keep you on track.*

Chapter Five

ATTITUDE IS EVERYTHING

- **If you want to live your best life now, you must have an attitude of gratitude.**

   I want to share a little story with you about the importance of *Speaking Truth to Your Own Heart.*[1]

Your attitude can be a cheerleader which leads you to happiness and success, or it can be an irate fan which causes you to be ejected from the game. There is a story that has been passed down through many generations of wise men called *Speak Truth to Your Own Heart.*[1]

There was a man who lived in a city called *Heaven Here on Earth*, the man's name was *They're Out to Get Me! Heaven Here on Earth* was a thriving and beautiful city with endless opportunities and some of the loveliest people you'd ever want to meet. People would go out of their way to give you a helping hand if you needed one.

They're Out to Get Me had a nickname he had given himself called *Nobody Likes Me.* One day *Nobody Likes Me* decided he would leave *Heaven Here on Earth* because he was fed up with the people in this city and wanted to find a better place to live. He searched the map and scratched his head. His finger moved quickly all over the map and found a new city. He suddenly felt in his heart he had found the right place. He got up early the next morning, packed his bags, loaded the car and struck out to get a fresh start.

The new city he had selected to live in was called *They Will Understand.* As he approached the city he stopped to gas up. The attendant came out with a big smile on his face to fill his car. As he pulled back the lid and unscrewed the cap to the

---

1 *Speak Truth to Your own Heart*: Written by Stephen F. Brown

gas tank *Nobody Likes Me* began to tell him how terrible his experience had been in the city he just left. He went up one side and down the other telling him how horrible the city and its people were. The gas attendant patiently listened. The man finally ended his description of *Heaven Here On Earth* with a question. He asked the attendant, "What do you think the people will be like in *They Will Understand?*" The attendant replied with a "Here we go again" attitude as he continued filling his tank; "Probably just like the city you just left." The moral of the story is **Attitude Is Everything.** The people living in *Heaven Here On Earth* did not need to change, the man needed to change his attitude. Your attitude is a stepping stone to happiness. A thankful attitude leads to a joyful life.

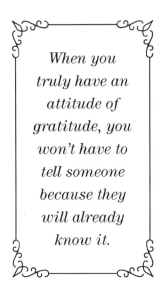

When you truly have an attitude of gratitude, you won't have to tell someone because they will already know it.

When you truly have an attitude of gratitude, you won't have to tell someone because they will already know it.

Psalm 28:7 (NLT) *The LORD is my strength and shield. I trust him with all my heart. He helps me, and my heart is filled with joy. I burst out in songs of thanksgiving.*

I Thessalonians 5:18 (NLT) *No matter what happens, always be thankful, for this is God's will for you who belong to Christ Jesus.*

- **If you want to live your best life now, you must watch what you say.**
  Being careful about the words you allow to come out of your mouth is huge with your heavenly Father.

Ephesians 4:29 (NCV) *When you talk, do not say harmful things, but say what people need—words that will help others become stronger. Then what you say will do good to those who listen to you.*

Your words can pollute or purify. If you constantly complain, you release poison into your life. There is an ancient Chinese Folk Saying that says: *It's better to light a candle than to curse the darkness.* How many of you know when you allow your life to be filled with complaining you harm your own life more than others? After you have dumped a bucket full of complaints on someone, you are the one who walks away angry, hurt, frustrated and upset. Believe me, it's not worth it!

Complaining is not based on your circumstances; it's based on the attitude of your heart. Remember, the Bible teaches us that out of the abundance of the heart the mouth speaks. You can turn the table on the devil by maintaining the right attitude during times of adversity. Stand back and watch God bless you. Remember, the Bible says "Give no place to the devil." The devil can't have a place unless you give him one. When you have a heart full of thanksgiving, it leaves no room for complaining or putting down others. There is always something to thank God for no matter what kind of adversity you may be facing in life, or what your life looks like. Start by thanking God for giving you life and salvation through Jesus Christ. Thank Him for the air you breathe and the sunsets you enjoy every day. Thank Him for His Spirit which dwells inside you. Thank God for whatever measure of health you have, it could be worse. Thank Him for the promises in His Word which teach us no matter where you are in life, He is leading you, guiding you and prospering you. Decide today to live a life of thanksgiving. Don't allow the poison of complaining to prevent you from receiving all God has for you!

- **Be joyful always, joyfulness is an attitude.**
- **Be joyful even when you don't feel like it.**

Acts 2:28 (TEV) *You have shown me the paths that lead to life, and your presence will fill me with joy.*

In Psalms, David said, I will bless the Lord at all times. His praise shall continually be in my mouth. At all times means in the good times as well as the tough times. It's easy to praise God when everything is going your way, but how do we handle it when adversity comes? The Bible tells us to stay full of joy no matter what we are going through in life. The winds of darkness may blow; things may become difficult and hard, but the Bible says remain joyful. The joy of the Lord is the source of our strength and the enemy knows it. He knows if he can steal your joy he's got you where he wants you. The devil knows if he can get you down and discouraged, before long you will become weak and feeble and he will be able to easily defeat you. Look at yourself in the mirror and say, *I will not become the devil's next meal.* When you are full of joy and have a good attitude, you keep yourself strong.

> *Decide today to live a life of thanksgiving. Don't allow the poison of complaining to prevent you from receiving all God has for you!*

Maintaining a positive attitude of faith paves the way for God to work miracles in your life and it is also a way for you to keep your foot on the devil's neck. Maintaining a positive attitude paves the way for God to turn bad situations around! Decide today to cultivate a good attitude. Keep yourself full of His joy by meditating on God's goodness and promises. When you do, you will soon experience supernatural strength and discover the victorious life God has promised you. Keep speaking faith words in your heart and watch God work things out in your behalf.

Chapter Summary

Neh. 8:10 (KJV) *the joy of the Lord is your strength.*

Practice repeating these words again and again to yourself, *the joy of the Lord is my strength, the joy of the Lord is my strength,* and joy and strength will be your friends for life.

Chapter Six

THINK THE WAY GOD THINKS

- **Everybody Likes Winners**

ABC's Wide World of Sports used to come on with the words, "The Thrill of Victory and the Agony of Defeat." There is nothing more exciting than winning. The sweet taste of victory is something we all desire. Everybody has visions of seeing themselves standing in the winner's circle with their arms raised high in victory. Victory is essential to our health, happiness and well-being. Defeat, on the other hand, triggers images of failure, lows, and not measuring up to the expectations of ourselves and others. None of us desire to experience that kind of pain.

Wallowing in defeat is even worse because it will eventually destroy your faith. It's not God's will for you to live a life of defeat, but it is His will for you to rise up and stand tall in the midst of Satan's attacks and live the victorious life God has provided for us.

1 Corinthians 15:57 (AMP) *But thanks be to God, Who gives us the victory [making us conquerors] through our Lord Jesus Christ.*

To live in victory you must think **victorious thoughts**. If you want to live your best life now you must realize, whether you think you can or think you can't, you're right. How you view things has everything to do with how you feel about yourself.

- **If you want to live your best life now, you must filter your thoughts.**

Filtering your thoughts means you don't let anything and everything pass through your mind. Filtering your thoughts means you are selective about what you allow yourself to meditate on.

Philip. 4:7 (GW) *Then God's peace, which goes beyond anything we can imagine, will guard your thoughts and emotions through Christ Jesus.*

Filtering our thoughts means we use the spiritual weapons Jesus has given us to dismantle and destroy Satan's attempt to control our thought life.

II Cor. 10:5 (MSG) *We use our powerful God-tools for smashing warped philosophies, tearing down barriers erected against the truth of God, fitting every loose thought and emotion and impulse into the structure of life shaped by Christ.*

Filtering your thoughts means you must set your spirit as a watchman over everything you allow yourself to see, hear, and do. This would include things like the movies we watch, the books we read, and the places we go. If you want to live your best life now, you must allow Jesus Christ to become Lord over these areas. What we see affects us more than we realize. David, the author of the book of Psalms, realized this timeless truth.

Psalm 101:3a (NCV) *I will not look at anything wicked.*

What you see affects how you think, how you think determines your actions, and your actions turn into a lifestyle. How you think determines your quality of life. The Bible encourages us to think on things which are pure, wholesome, and of good report **(Phil 4:8)**.

- **When you keep your thoughts on good things, good things will follow.**
  Proverbs 22:11 (NCV) *Whoever loves pure thoughts and kind words will have even the king as a friend.*

In order to think on right things, you must filter what you watch, what you read, what you hear, and where you go. Don't let the enemy slowly deceive you into lowering your standards and no longer becoming sensitive to what is good, pure and true. Don't allow yourself to be deceived the way the Galatians were.

Galatians 3:1 (MSG) *You crazy Galatians! Did someone put a hex on you? Have you taken leave of your senses? Something crazy has happened, for it's obvious that you no longer have the crucified Jesus in clear focus in your lives. His sacrifice on the Cross was certainly set before you clearly enough.*

Don't let the devil have a single opportunity to pull you down by watching or being involved in things that are questionable. Remember you are the temple of the Holy Spirit. Fill your thoughts with the promises found in God's Word to bless you, protect you, and lead you into every good path and right direction. Set your thoughts on God's promises of freedom, peace, safety and deliverance. As you fill your thoughts with God's Word, victory will come alive in every area of your life!

> *It's not God's will for you to live a life of defeat, but it is His will for you to rise up and stand tall in the midst of Satan's attacks and live the victorious life God has provided for us.*

- **God wants you to learn how to think the way He thinks**
  1 Cor. 2:9 (TLB) says: *That is what is meant by the Scriptures which say that no mere man has ever seen, heard, or even imagined what wonderful things God has ready for those who love the Lord.*

  Philip. 4:8 (NCV) *Brothers and sisters, think about the things that are good and worthy of praise. Think about the* *things that are true and honorable and right and pure and beautiful and respected. No matter where you are in life right now, God has much more in store for you.*

God wants to take you to new levels in every area of your life. He wants to give you more wisdom so you may make better decisions. He wants to give you a stronger anointing so you can have greater influence. He wants to bless you financially so you can be a blessing to others. Don't get stuck in the same old rut of believing life is caving in all around you, there's so much more to life than that. Dare to believe our God is a God of more than enough and more than able to meet your needs whatever they may be.

The Cruise Ship Story[2]

Let me tell you a story about a man named Jake in a faraway country who dreamed about going to America to build a better life for himself. Growing up, his parents had told him that America was a land of hope and opportunity. Jake's thoughts were imprisoned for several years with hopes about going to America to fulfill his dreams. He was convinced if he could just make it to America all his prayers would be answered and he would have a better life. Jake was not a wealthy man by any stretch of imagination, but he saved his money diligently to fulfill his dream. The day finally came when he had saved enough money to buy a ticket on a cruise ship to America. Because he had to spend most of his money for his ticket, he knew he would not have money to buy expensive meals. The way he decided to solve this problem was to buy a bunch of peanut butter and crackers to eat on his two week cruise. The day he had worked and saved for so hard had

---

2 *The cruise ship story based on " Your Best Life Now" - by Joel Osteen*

finally come and he found himself walking across the boarding ramp to the cruise ship with his luggage in tow, along with his carefully packed peanut butter and crackers. He reached out and handed the attendant his ticket with a big smile on his face. His mind and heart were filled with excitement and joy because his hopes and dreams were about to become a reality.

After everyone had boarded the ship he was directed to his quarters along with the other 150 passengers. His room was a bit small with no window, but that was OK because he was finally on his way to America. Each day the passengers would gather together in the dining hall to eat wonderfully prepared delicious meals. Jake didn't have much money because he had spent most of what he had saved on his ticket. So each day at meal time he would sit in a corner, pull out his peanut butter and crackers, and eat them while the other passengers ate till they could eat no more. Jake would sit there smelling the aroma of all the good food and watching all the other passengers enjoying it as he ate his peanut butter and crackers.

Don't let the enemy slowly deceive you into lowering your standards and no longer becoming sensitive to what is good, pure and true.

This went on for days and they were now in the eleventh day of the two week cruise. Dinner time had come once again and as usual all the passengers except Jake gathered in the dining hall to eat. Jake once again sat in the corner all alone and ate his peanut butter and crackers. One of the passengers walked over to him and said, *"Sir do you mind if I ask you a question?"* Jake said, *"Sure go ahead."* The man went on to say, *"Why have you been sitting here day after day all alone eating peanut butter and crackers?"* With a flushed expression of embarrassment on his face, Jake begins to explain to the man how he spent most his money on his ticket and did not have enough money to buy expensive meals like the other passengers. The man looked at Jake with an expression of bewilderment on his face and said; *"Man, don't you realize all the meals were included free with the ticket you bought?"* Jake jumped up, left the man standing there without saying a word, and ran into the dining hall and began to enjoy all the delicious food with the other passengers.

What is moral of this story? When you give your life to Jesus, all the meals are paid for by the blood Jesus shed for us at Calvary, and you don't have to sit in the corner of life and eat peanut butter and crackers. You can go to the dining hall and eat from the table of the abundant supply provided by the Holy Spirit. You don't have to beg and plead for God to bless you. When you give your life to Jesus you are invited to eat all you want while the devil watches.

Psalm 23:5 (KJV) *Thou preparest a table before me in the presence of mine enemies: thou anointest my head with oil; my cup runneth over.*

Chapter Summary

Never forget since Jesus is alive and actively involved in the lives of His people, there is yet hope and victory. God has new frontiers for you to explore and higher mountains for you to climb, and wider rivers for you to cross! You still have many new opportunities to be used by God, if you will allow Him to use you. It does not matter how young or old you are, or what stage in life you may be in, dare to believe God that your best days are in front of you. Begin today to think the way God thinks.

The Bible says the path of the righteous grows brighter and brighter, not darker and darker. Dare to think increase, dare to think abundance, dare to see God blessing you! Dare to think bigger than you are thinking right now, dare to let your mind soar to places you never thought possible. See yourself at the helm of Starship Enterprise with a mission from God to go where no man has gone before!

Chapter Seven

SEE YOURSELF AS GOD SEES YOU

- **If you want to live your best life now, you must see yourself as God sees you. If you are to see yourself as God sees you, you must raise your self-image.**

Let's take a look in God's Word at Gideon and his struggles with self-image.

Judges 6: 12 (NIV) *When the angel of the Lord appeared to Gideon, he said, "The Lord is with you, mighty warrior."*

Judges 6: 15 *"But Lord," Gideon asked, "how can I save Israel? My clan is the weakest in Manasseh, and I am the least in my family."*

You must learn to see yourself the way God sees you. The Bible says, "As a man thinks in his heart, so is he." In the King James translation God called Gideon a '**mighty man of valor**' because that's how God saw him. In the New Living Translation he is called a '**mighty hero**.' When God called Gideon *A mighty man of valor*, Gideon turned around and said, *who me?* Again you must learn how to see yourself the way God sees you. It's important that each of us learn how to make our speech match what the Word of God says about us. The Bible teaches us to change what we are looking at and believing for. You must believe God is for you and desires good things for your life and then step back and watch it happen. If you choose to stay focused on negative

> *You must believe God is for you and desires good things for your life and then step back and watch it happen.*

things in your life, then by your own choice you are agreeing with the enemy.

- **The decisions you make in life will cast the deciding vote which in turn will determine your happiness and the outcome of your future.**

You are the artist, the brush is in your hand and you are the one who decides what the picture of your life will look like.

God gave Joshua and the children of Israel the same choice for peace and happiness He's giving to you and me today. Joshua told them to choose life, and God is telling us to do the same thing, choose life!

> *The way you choose life is to believe what God's Word says about the outcome of your life more than what the naysayers and the devil are trying to make you believe.*

Deut. 30:19 (NLT) *"Today I have given you the choice between life and death, between blessings and curses. I call on heaven and earth to witness the choice you make. Oh, that you would choose life, that you and your descendants might live!"*

The way you choose life is to believe what God's Word says about the outcome of your life more than what the naysayers and the devil are trying to make you believe. Dare to tell the devil he's a liar, don't believe a word he says. The Bible says, *"Give no place to the devil."* When you believe the devil's lies over God's Word, it opens doors of destruction in your life. But on the other hand, if you choose to agree with God and His Word, you can turn things around in your favor once and for all. This will only happen when you begin to see yourself the way God sees you.

Chapter Summary

Choose the way of blessing.

Psalm 119:30 (KJV) *I have chosen the way of truth: thy judgments have I laid before me.*

Chapter Eight

LET JESUS SHAPE YOUR LIFE

- **If you want to live your best life now, let Jesus shape your thoughts.**

    II Cor. 10:5 (MSG) *We use our powerful God-tools for smashing warped philosophies, tearing down barriers erected against the truth of God, fitting every loose thought and emotion and impulse into the structure of life shaped by Christ.*

The Bible has a lot to say about allowing Jesus Christ to shape your life. One of the best-selling religious books written by Joel Osteen a few years ago was *Your Best Life Now.* When I read this book I was greatly blessed by it. In fact, that's where I gleaned the title for this book says, "God wants this to be the best time of your life."[3]

And that's absolutely true if you are a Christian, but if you are not, you are in big trouble. Many Christians are divided about whether or not a believer can live their best life now. Some believe we must wait until we get to heaven before we can receive the blessings, joy, and happiness we seek. Some church leaders say we can have all the blessings we want now. I believe both camps of thought have a measure of truth. From what I understand about Scripture, the truth is somewhere in the middle. In **Job 14:1 (KJV) it says:** *Man that is born of a woman is of few days, and full of trouble.*

So it's obvious our existence in this life is not a cakewalk, without any problems.

In fact in **I Peter 4:12** it says: *Beloved, think it not strange concerning the fiery trial which is to try you, as though some strange thing happened unto you.*

In this life every follower of Christ can expect to experience

---

3   Osteen, Joel: *Your Best Life Now*, page 5

mountain top and valley experiences at one time or another. Sometimes we may even experience them both in the same day. But the Bible teaches us that by applying the principles of faith we can level the playing field, and live life above our problems.

Living your best life now doesn't mean you won't experience trouble in life, it simply means we have been mandated by God to apply the principles of faith and actively seek the best God has for us in the mist of trouble.

Isaiah 40:4 (AMP) *Every valley shall be lifted and filled up, and every mountain and hill shall be made low; and the crooked and uneven shall be made straight and level, and the rough places a plain.*

Living your best life now doesn't mean you won't experience trouble in life, it simply means we have been mandated by God to apply the principles of faith and actively seek the best God has for us in the mist of trouble. Not tomorrow, not next week, not next month, not next year, but right now. If you aren't believing God to bless you now, it's not faith. Faith is always now.

Hebrews 11:1 (KJV) *Now faith is the substance of things hoped for, the evidence of things not seen.*

To show you how little respect God has for the devil, God feeds us with spiritual food while the devil stands right there looking. David said God prepared a table for him in the presence of his enemies.

The way we think about things determine how we believe.

Proverbs 4:23 (TEV) *Be careful how you think; your life is shaped by your thoughts.*

The Bible tells us *as a man thinketh in his heart, so is he.* No matter what you are going through in your life, no matter how many disappointments or setbacks you have suffered, hold on, new victories are just around the corner. You may not understand everything you are going through, but stay positive, knowing there is always hope with God on your side. Someone once said *"If God is for us who can be against us?"*

You are a King's kid so hold your head high, knowing God is in your corner, He is in control, and He is working behind the scenes causing all things to work together for your good. Your dreams may not have turned out exactly the way you hoped, but don't give up; God's plan for your life is still unfolding. God knows your value; and sees your potential.

He will never give up on you, so don't give up on yourself.

- **If you want to live your best life now, you must develop a vision of victory.**
  Isaiah 43:19 (GW) *I am going to do something new. It is already happening. Don't you recognize it? I will clear a way in the desert. I will make rivers on dry land.*

Do you perceive victory in your every step? Are you living each day filled with faith and expectations of God's blessing? Are you believing God's best is knocking on the door of your life right now?

Isaiah 43:19 didn't say God would do it next week, or maybe next month, or even next year. No! God said I'm doing something new in your life right now! Then God asked Isaiah the question, *"Don't you recognize it?"*

Have you ever stopped to look around and see what God is doing in your life? I guarantee you if you do, you will begin to recognize God is still in the blessing business. Sometimes we have to slow down and get quiet before we can see the Hand of God working in our lives. God wants to do something new in your life today, will you allow Him, will you let Him, will you dare to believe it?

We had a saying when I was a kid, to challenge someone to do something daring. We would say, *"I dare you to do it, I double dog dare you."* And I double dog dare you to take a step onto the waters of faith, into the uncharted waters of God! It's time, like never before, to let go of your old way of thinking which has been holding you back from becoming all God wants you to be. Dare to take hold of the new thing God has in front of you! God said in **Jeremiah 29:11**, *My plans for you are good and not evil, to give you a future and a hope.*

> *You may not understand everything you are going through, but stay positive, knowing there is always hope with God on your side.*

God's plans for you are good, regardless of what has happened in your past, or how things may look or appear around you. No matter the setbacks or tragedies you have experienced in the past; God is working behind the scene this very moment on your behalf. God wants to give you a better life. He wants you to know the blessings He has for you are not based on what others think or do. No, God bases your blessings on how you think and what you do. God wants you to know the ball is in your court as to whether or not you are blessed by Him.

Settle in your mind that the devil or other people can't stop God from blessing you. When you make an honest effort to find God, you can't help being blessed. The blessings of God will come your way like a runaway freight train coming down a steep hill with no brakes. God will cause all things to work together for your good when you seek His plan for your life and develop a vision for victory.

How you respond in the midst of difficult situations has a direct impact on the outcome.

- **Expect God's Favor**
- **Expect to be blessed, expect things to change in your favor.**

Be strong-willed, stand your ground, be determined and do everything you can to recover what the enemy has stolen.

II Thes. 2:15 (MSG) *So, friends, take a firm stand, feet on the ground and head high. Keep a tight grip on what you were taught, whether in personal conversation or by our letter.*

Remember, obstacles are simply opportunities for advancement.

If you'll do your part to have a restoration mentality, God will do His.

- **Expect God's Favor In Every Area of Life.**
  We have just looked at how Job found favor with God, and God put a hedge of protection around him. Noah also found favor with God: In **Gen. 6:8** it says: *But Noah found favor in the eyes of the LORD.* The Bible teaches that the godly are showered with blessings.

Proverbs 10:6a (NLT) says: *The godly are showered with blessings.*

In **Psalms 84:11 (KJV)** David said: *The Lord bestows favor and honor, no good thing does He withhold from those whose walk is blameless.*

> *The blessings of God will come your way like a runaway freight train coming down a steep hill with no brakes.*

What an awesome promise – no good thing will He withhold. God also wants to pour out His abundant blessings, His abundant victory, and abundant favor in your life! In **Psalm 8:5** the Bible says, *God has crowned us with glory and honor.* Another word for honor is favor. In other words, God has crowned us with His favor! He wants you to thrive and excel in life. You are a child of the most-high God. You walk in His favor each and every day; not because of who you are, but because of whose you are! You are highly favored because you are a child of God and He wants you to be favor-minded. To be favor-minded simply means that you are releasing your faith, knowing God wants to bless you.

- Turn to yourself and say: *The more favor-minded I am, the more of God's favor I am going to attract!*

Begin to declare you have favor with God. Knowing God's favor will bring you to a place of peace, hope, and victory like you've never experienced before.

- **Expect To Be Blessed**
  If you want to live your best life now, you must expect good things to happen in your life.

Psalm 84:11 (TLB) *For Jehovah God is our Light and our Protector. He gives us grace and glory.*
No good thing will he withhold from those who walk along his paths.

What are you expecting in life; good things? Bad things? Big things? Little things? Are you expecting God to do something big in your life? If you're not, you should be. God wants you to get your hopes up. He wants you to hope big in Him. God wants you to never let go of hope.

Remember, obstacles are simply opportunities for advancement.

Psalm 71:14 (CEV) *I will never give up hope or stop praising you.*

Your expectations set the limit for your life.

Poem – I Bargained With Life
I bargained with life for a penny, and life would pay no more.

For life is just an employer, which pays you what you ask and no more. It's up to you to set your price, and life will pay you what is right. What is right is up to you.

By Stephen F. Brown

If you never expect to be blessed in life, you won't be. If you never expect anything good, you won't receive anything good. If you don't expect things to get better, they won't. God promises to meet you at your level of expectancy. That's why Jesus said in **Matthew 9:29** (NLT), *Because of your faith, it will happen.* Another translation says, *Have what your faith expects.* Expect the blessings of God to overcome beyond your wildest dreams.

Eph. 3:20 (MSG) *God can do anything, you know—far more than you could ever imagine or guess or request in your wildest dreams! He does it not by pushing us around but by working within us, his Spirit deeply and gently within us.*

- **If you want to live your best life now, you must believe your God will take care of you.**
  Matthew 6:26 (CEV) *Look at the birds in the sky! They don't plant or harvest. They don't even store grain in barns. Yet your Father in heaven takes care of them. Aren't you worth more than birds?*

- Trust God to lead you to new victories in Christ.
  I John 5:4 (NLT) *For every child of God defeats this evil world by trusting Christ to give the victory.*

Your expectations set the limit for your life.

As a child of God, you have the power within you to overcome the world.

I John 4:4 (KJV) *Ye are of God, little children, and have overcome them: because greater is he that is in you, than he that is in the world.*

That includes everything in the world, and everything the world brings your way. Always remember nothing is too tough or too hard with God on your side. Living your best life now is not running from trouble but rather facing it head on.

- If you want to live your best life now allow God to bless you. That's right! Get yourself out of the way and let God bless you. How many of you know sometimes we are the biggest stumbling block in the way that is preventing God from blessing us? Get out of the way and let God bless you.

Psalm 37:4 (MSG) *Keep company with GOD, get in on the best.*

Psalm 37:4 (ESV) *Delight yourself in the LORD, and he will give you the desires of your heart.*

Three Stepping Stones to God's Blessings

God's blessings come from three sources:

1. Grace
2. God's wisdom
3. Our actions - put legs on your prayers.

- **If you want to live your best life now, you must Release your Past.**
  Phil 3:13-14 (NIV) *Brothers, I do not consider myself yet to have taken hold of it. But one thing I do: Forgetting what is behind and straining toward what is ahead, 14 I press on toward the goal to win the prize for which God has called me heavenward in Christ Jesus.*

One of the main keys to overcoming disappointments in life is learning to let go of the past. You let go of the past by choosing to forgive those who have hurt you, or wronged you. The way you do this is by believing God will restore to you anything that was taken or lost. When you receive Christ's forgiveness in your life, you are released from the pressure to make up for past mistakes or failures. Don't let the regrets of yesterday destroy your hopes for tomorrow. No matter what has happened in the past, God is a God of restoration and He will restore what the enemy has stolen from you.

God promises to meet you at your level of expectancy.

Proverbs 6:31 (CEV) *And thieves who get caught must pay back seven times what was stolen and lose everything.*

God wants you to start experiencing the bright future He has in store for you. Don't let the regrets of yesterday destroy the hopes of tomorrow. Accept God's mercy and forgiveness today, and look forward to the wonderful plan He has for your future!

Jeremiah 29:11 (NIV) *For I know the plans I have for you," declares the LORD, "plans to prosper you and not to harm you, plans to give you hope and a future."*

- **Declare You Are Blessed!**
  Numbers 6:23-26 (NLT) [23] *"Tell Aaron and his sons to bless the people of Israel with this special blessing:* [24] *'May the LORD bless you and protect you.* [25] *May the LORD smile on you and be gracious to you.* [26] *May the LORD show you his favor and give you his peace.'*

> *Living your best life now is not running from trouble but rather facing it head on.*

A blessing is not a blessing until it is declared! So today, declare a blessing over yourself and others. Speak that blessing in the name of Jesus! Declare you are blessed with God's supernatural wisdom and receive clear direction for your life. Declare today that you are blessed with creativity, courage, talent and abundance.

Declare today you are the head and not the tail, declare you are above and not beneath. Declare God's blessings and wisdom over your finances. Declare you are blessed with a strong will, self-control and self-discipline.

Declare you are blessed with a great family, good friends, and good health. Declare you are blessed with good success, supernatural strength, promotion and divine protection. Declare you are blessed with a compassionate heart and a positive outlook on life.

Declare that any curse or negative word that has ever been spoken over you is broken right now in the name of Jesus. Declare that everything you put your hands to is going to prosper and succeed.

- **Declare You Have The Mind of Christ.**
  Philippians 2:5-6 (KJV) *Let this mind be in you, which was also in Christ Jesus: ⁶ Who, being in the form of God, thought it not robbery to be equal with God.*

- **Develop A Restoration Mentality**.
  Exodus 22:7 (NIV) *"If a man gives his neighbor silver or goods for safekeeping and they are stolen from the neighbor's house, the thief, if he is caught, must pay back double."*

Joel 2:25 (TEV) *I will give you back what you lost in the years when swarms of locusts ate your crops.*

In verse *25* God told Israel, *"I will restore the years that the locusts have eaten and I will bring you out with plenty and you shall be satisfied."* God wants you to live a happy and satisfied life. He has promised to restore all the things the enemy has stolen.

However, just because God gives this great promise doesn't mean it will

> *Declare today you are the head and not the tail, declare you are above and not beneath. Declare God's blessings and wisdom over your finances.*

automatically come your way like ripe cherries falling off a tree. You have to do your part to develop a restoration mindset.

Philippians 2:5-6 (KJV) *Let this mind be in you, which was also in Christ Jesus: ⁶ Who, being in the form of God, thought it not robbery to be equal with God.*

- **Declare What You Believe**

- **If you want to live your best life now, you must speak what you want. Declare what is to be!**
  Isaiah 45:21 (NIV) *Declare what is to be, present it--let them take counsel together. Who foretold this long ago, who declared it from the distant past? Was it not I, the LORD? And there is no God apart from me, a righteous God and a Savior; there is none but me.*

If you're going to live a life of victory, you must speak positive words of faith and declare what God says about your situation.

> *Declare today you are the head and not the tail, declare you are above and not beneath. Declare God's blessings and wisdom over your finances.*

Philippians 4:13 declares that you can do all things through Christ who strengthens you.

If you want to live your best life now, you must learn how to say about yourself what the Word of God says about you. No matter how inadequate or unqualified you may feel, Jesus promised to strengthen and empower you. When the time of adversity comes, what do you say about your situation? Do you declare that you are about to go under any minute, or do you declare,

I can do all things through Christ who infuses me with new strength? Anyone can be positive when things are going well. Anyone can remain positive when everyone is patting you on the back and telling you what a great guy you are. But the way you respond when adversity comes will make or break you. The world has a saying; *the proof is in the pudding.*

> *Don't look at the facts of your situation; look at the truths found in God's Word.*

Your Christian maturity is proven to yourself, and the entire world by how you handle the test and trials of everyday life. How you respond in the midst of difficult situations has a direct impact on the outcome. Don't look at the facts of your situation; look at the truths found in God's Word. Declare His truth over your situation until the facts line up with God's Word.

II Cor. 4:13 (MSG) *We're not keeping this quiet, not on your life. Just like the psalmist who wrote, "I believed it, so I said it," we say what we believe.*

Put the enemy on the run with your tongue by speaking faith-filled words.

Numbers 10:35 (KJV) *And it came to pass, when the ark set forward, that Moses said, Rise up, Lord, and let thine enemies be scattered; and let them that hate thee flee before thee.*

- **If you want to live your best life now, you must declare You Have Spiritual Strength.**

Joel 3:10 says, *let the weak say I am strong.*

You must not be afraid to tell the devil you have spiritual strength.

Luke 10:19 (KJV) *Behold, I give unto you power to tread on serpents and scorpions, and over all the power of the enemy: and nothing shall by any means hurt you.*

Chapter Summary

Every believer must learn how to fight spiritual warfare somewhere along the way. That includes you and me. It includes those who feel like fighting and those who don't.

Joel 3:10 states, *even the weak must fight.*

Chapter Nine

GUARD YOUR HEART

- **If you want to remain joyful and productive for God, you must guard Your Heart.**

In **Psalms 119** David said, *thy word have I hid in my heart that I might not sin against thee.* Hiding God's Word in our heart conveys the thought or idea of putting God's Word in a place the devil can't get it. The heart of a tree is found in the center of the tree. The center of the tree is the furthest place from its outer edge. Hiding the Word of God in our hearts represents the furthest place from Satan's reach. Guarding your heart is one of the most important responsibilities given to every believer.

Proverbs 4:23 (GW) *Guard your heart more than anything else, because the source of your life flows from it.*

Proverbs 4:23 (NLT) *Above all else, guard your heart, for it affects everything you do.*

Let's take a look at a verse of Scripture from the parable of the sower that teaches us an important lesson about our heart as a type of spiritual soil which receives the seed of God's Word.

> *Guarding your heart is one of the most important responsibilities given to every believer.*

Matthew 13:22 (MSG) *"The seed cast in the weeds is the person who hears the kingdom news, but weeds of worry and illusions about getting more and wanting everything under the sun strangle what was heard, and nothing comes of it.*

In this story, Jesus tells how the enemy comes to steal the seed of God's Word through temptations, cares of this life, and anxieties. God is constantly trying to plant new seeds of victory in the soil of our hearts. If you harbor bitterness, jealousy, or pride in your

Keeping strife out of your life is a vital key to living the abundant life God has in store for you!

heart, God's Word won't be able to take root and develop in your life. You are good ground for the seed of God's Word to grow when you guard your heart by standing and believing God's promises will come to pass – even when the circumstances don't agree. Don't allow circumstances and discouragement to affect your faith. Post your spirit man as a guard to your heart, knowing through faith and patience you will inherit all the things God has promised you!

Hebrews 10:36 (MSG) *But you need to stick it out, staying with God's plan so you'll be there for the promised completion.*

- **If you want to live your best life now, you must know when to let go.**
  Abraham Lincoln: *When you have got an elephant by the leg, and he is trying to run away, it's best to let him go.*

If you want to live your best life now, you must learn when to let go of people who don't want your help, or God's help!

- **Don't let others sink your ship or steal your joy**
  Most of you are familiar with the story about the Titanic which hit an iceberg and sunk at sea. If you allow it, others in life can become like the iceberg that sank the Titanic. They will cause you to crash and also sink your ship. I have a saying that states *don't let yourself become a part of another man's darkness.* Each of us must learn where to draw a line in life when relationships clearly become unhealthy for us! It's better to bite one bullet today, than a dozen tomorrow, don't be afraid to speak up!

- **If you want to find true happiness you must run from the works of the flesh like a plague!**
  James 3:16 (CEV) *Whenever people are jealous or selfish, they cause trouble and do all sorts of cruel things.*

Do you seem to have an invisible wall preventing you from experiencing God's blessing and favor? If you do, maybe it's because you have allowed strife to creep in. The Bible tells us when we hold on to strife, it brings confusion and trouble of all sorts. Strife opens the door to every evil work of the enemy.

Strife can creep in like a cancer to steal your peace, destroy relationships, and extinguish hope. You must constantly stay on guard against strife and make the decision to walk in love and peace. Keeping strife out of your life is a vital key to living the abundant life God has in store for you! Follow the example of Jesus and let your words and actions bring life to those around you.

Chapter Summary

Focus more on loving people than proving your point. It's better to be kind than it is to be right. God wants us to learn that being kind is more important than always feeling the need to prove we are right all the time. As you honor and prefer others and lay your own opinions aside, you'll discover a level of peace you never experienced before. You will find yourself enjoying new levels of victory and abundance! Our purpose or reason for existing is to love God and His Church. God wants us to join Him in His mission to fix a lost and hurting world by demonstrating His love. Live a life that shows the love of God is shed abroad in our hearts by the Holy Spirit.

Chapter Ten

REFUSE TO WORRY

When I look at the world around me, I see people worrying in every area of life 24/7. Believe it or not, even our children have worries.

What is Worry?

A simple and practical definition for worry is *excessive concern for something we cannot change*. The New Testament Greek word for worry means *to divide, part, rip, or tear*. These are just a few words which describe the effects of worry. Let's take a look at what the Bible has to say about worry.

Proverbs 12:25 (MSG) *Worry weighs us down; a cheerful word picks us up.*

Philip. 4:6 (MSG) *Don't fret or worry. Instead of worrying, pray. Let petitions and praises shape your worries into prayers, letting God know your concerns.*

Worry is a powerful and destructive force which can stop you from fulfilling your God-given destiny, so it's important that you and I learn to resist the temptation to worry.

Isaiah 2:3 says: *God will keep those in perfect peace who keep their minds stayed on Him.*

When you worry you are doing the exact opposite of what the Scripture says. Instead of focusing on God and His power, we are fixing our minds on what the enemy is telling us about our problems. We can't stop Satan from pointing out our problems, but we can refuse to focus on them. We can refuse to entertain them. One way to do this is by casting all of our cares and concerns on Jesus.

Decide today to put an end to worry in your life.

- **If you want to live your best life now, you must give Jesus all your worries.**
  I Peter 5:7 (NLT) *Give all your worries and cares to God, for he cares about what happens to you.*

Many people think worry is a normal part of everyday life, and unavoidable, but nothing could be further from the truth. God doesn't want you to live a life filled with worry. Worry weighs down our spirit and damages our physical bodies. We lose sleep, we lose weight, our hair falls out and the story goes on and on.

When you allow worry to set in, it steals your peace, your joy, your sleep, your health, and affects every area of your life. Worry steals precious moments of time that you can never get back. As you focus on God's Word, you'll drive out every attempt of the devil to steal your peace and joy. You will experience the fulfillment of God's promises as never before. Decide today to put an end to worry in your life. Don't feed worry by focusing on bad news all the time.

Feed your spirit faith food by meditating on God's Word and filling your heart and mind with God's promises. Declare every day is a good day because you belong to God. Declare, *My God shall supply all of my needs according to His riches and glory.* Declare, *My God makes a way out of no way and is the Restorer and Redeemer of my soul.* Make no mistake about worry; it is not your friend. The Bible says, *the thief comes to steal, kill, and to destroy.* If worry is draining the life of God out of you, draw a line today and do something about it. Say to yourself, "Self, stop worrying and dare to live your best life now."

- **Praise God At All Times**

- **If you want to live your best life now, you must praise**

God in the good times and the bad times.
Nothing stirs the pot of joy in our hearts more than praise. If you want to see God move in your life when it seems like the devil has your back pinned against the wall, just start praising God. The following scriptures paint two of the most powerful pictures in the Bible about the power of praise.

II Chron. 20:21-24 (KJV) *And when he had consulted with the people, he appointed singers unto the Lord, and that should praise the beauty of holiness, as they went out before the army, and to say, Praise the Lord; for his mercy endureth forever. 22And when they began to sing and to praise, the Lord set ambushments against the children of Ammon, Moab, and mount Seir, which were come against Judah; and they were smitten. 23For the children of Ammon and Moab stood up against the inhabitants of mount Seir, utterly to slay and destroy them: and when they had made an end of the inhabitants of Seir, every one helped to destroy another. 24And when Judah came toward the watch tower in the wilderness, they looked unto the multitude, and, behold, they were dead bodies fallen to the earth, and none escaped.*

> *If you want to see God move in your life when it seems like the devil has your back pinned against the wall, just start praising God.*

Acts 16:22-26 (NLT) *A mob quickly formed against Paul and Silas, and the city officials ordered them stripped and beaten with wooden rods. 23They were severely beaten, and then they were thrown into prison. The jailer was ordered to make sure they didn't escape. 24So he took no chances but put them into the* *inner dungeon and clamped their feet in the stocks. [25]Around midnight, Paul and Silas were praying and singing hymns to God, and the other prisoners were listening. [26]Suddenly, there was a great earthquake, and the prison was shaken to its foundations. All the doors flew open, and the chains of every prisoner fell off!*

Chapter Summary

Praise and worship has always been a powerful conduit that leads into the presence of God. We can talk about Him, do things for Him, and even pray to Him, but it is only through praise and worship that we are allowed to be in the presence and power of our Lord and Savior Jesus Christ.

Chapter Eleven

KNOW GOD HAS APPROVED YOU

If you want to live your best life now, you must know **God Has Approved You**.

Jeremiah 1:5 (AMP) *Before you were ever formed in your mother's womb, I saw you and approved you.*

You are approved by Almighty God! Isn't that awesome? As the world says, "It doesn't get any better than that." You are created in His image, and you are the apple of His eye.

You are the sheep of His pasture. You are His son or daughter. As children of God, as the youth would say, "You've got swag!" You did not choose God, but He chose you and He is pleased with you. Notice Jeremiah didn't say God approves of you as long as you don't have any faults, or as long as you don't make any mistakes. No, it just simply said God approved him with no strings attached before he was born.

How many of you know that God loved us while we were yet sinners, God loves you just as you are? God's love for you is not based on what you do or don't do. That's why God's love is different and more powerful than any love mankind has ever known. God loves and approves you unconditionally. No matter how many weaknesses you think you have, no matter how many times you fall or mess up, get right back up again, hold your head up high and keep moving forward in God. There is a song by Donnie McClurkin called *We Fall*

> *No matter how many weaknesses you think you have, no matter how many times you fall or mess up, get right back up again, hold your head up high and keep moving forward in God.*

Down. In this song he talks about when followers of Christ fall into sin, they should not stay down. Don't stay there wallowing in sin, but rather get right back up, brush yourself off, purpose in your heart to live for God and keep right on pressing forward in God. Don't allow the enemy to bring strife into your life by deceiving you into thinking you are not good enough. You are as valuable in the eyes of God as the person sitting next to you and that's what matters; that's what counts. Stand strong in thoughts about yourself knowing you have been chosen and approved by God. God wants you to know He will finish the good work He began in you.

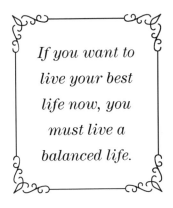

If you want to live your best life now, you must live a balanced life.

Philip. 1:6 (TLB) *And I am sure that God who began the good work within you will keep right on helping you grow in his grace until his task within you is finally finished on that day when Jesus Christ returns.*

- If you want to live your best life now, you must live a balanced life.
  Look yourself in the eyes and say, *"Blessed are the balanced for they will outlast all the rest."* It's a mistake to spend so much time helping others while your own life falls apart.

Song of Solomon 1:6d (KJV) *They made me the keeper of the vineyards; but mine own vineyard have I not kept.*

Are there areas of your life you have neglected because you are busy taking care of everyone else? If you're always on the go, constantly working to bless and help others and never taking time for yourself, you will end up stressed out and overwhelmed, and you won't be able to enjoy life the way God intended. Take time out to smell the roses and do something you enjoy. If you don't, in the end you won't be of much help to yourself or anybody else. God wants you to learn the value of living a balanced life. Living a balanced life brings peace, joy, health and happiness.

The person speaking in Song of Solomon was good at taking care of everyone else; his friends, his family, and his work. He made sure everyone else was happy, but in doing that, he neglected to take care of himself. Are you living like that today? Do you spend all your time helping other people, and having little or no time for yourself? I am preaching to the choir here! I am guilty of this, as I also know some of you are. If we don't do something, we are going to crash and burn ourselves out, and the smoke from the burning rubbish will be seen miles away. By no means am I saying we should not be concerned about the welfare of others. But what I am saying is we need to find the right balance. If you don't, people will use you up, until there's nothing left. And when you allow that to happen, everyone loses. Decide along with me today to begin investing time in yourself. It's great to bless and help others, but also invest some time in yourself.

> *When you are refreshed emotionally, physically, and spiritually, you are able to give to others more effectively.*

Take time out to relax and rejuvenate. When you are refreshed emotionally, physically, and spiritually, you are able to give to others more effectively.

As you bring balance to your life, you will begin to enjoy every day to the fullest, just the way God intended!

- **If you want to live your best life now, you must *obey* God's voice and His Word.**
  What a wise man does in the beginning, the fool does in the end.

  Isaiah 1:19 (KJV) *If ye be willing and obedient, ye shall eat the good of the land:*

  Isaiah 1:19 (MSG) *If you'll willingly obey, you'll feast like kings.*

- If you want to live your best life now, you must stand firm in God's truth.
  Exodus 14:13 (NIV) *Moses answered the people, "Do not be afraid. Stand firm and you will see the deliverance the Lord will bring you today. The Egyptians you see today you will never see again.*

If you want to live your best life now, you must take a stand on basic Bible principles which are true in God's Word. When you take a stand for truth, you make a declaration of your faith in God. This automatically raises your shield of faith which can extinguish all the flaming arrows of the evil one. When you step out to do something big for God, the enemy will send challenges and make every effort possible to distract you, and knock you off course. So take a stand today, and stay on the course the Lord has set for you.

- **If you are going to live your best life now, you must know God is with you.**
  Let's take a look at an example using Abraham and Lot. Having God on your side is like having *Hulk* on the right and *Luke*

Cage on the left and *Superman* flying out ahead. The Bible says, *if God be for us who can be against us.*

You'll be amazed at what God will do in your life when you stand your ground and face your challenges head on and hold your head up high and hold fast to the promises found in God's Word. When you take a stand like this for God, you are making a declaration of your faith which echoes throughout heaven and the Hall of Fame which faith filled believers have entered through all history.

Your decision to take a stand against the devil automatically raises your shield of faith which has the ability to extinguish all the flaming arrows of the evil one.

Ephesians 6:16 (KJV) *Above all, taking the shield of faith, wherewith ye shall be able to quench all the fiery darts of the wicked.*

So take a stand today, and stay on the course the Lord has set for you.

Chapter Summary

Take a stand in your prayer life. Take a stand in your Bible study time. Take a stand in developing a servant's heart. Take a stand in your marriage. Take a stand in your finances. Take a stand in extending acts of love and service to others. Take a stand by getting involved in finding something you can do to help build God's Kingdom. Take a stand today and watch God work in your life. Take a stand this day and see the salvation and provision of God become a living reality in every area of your life.

Chapter Twelve

PUT ON THE BOXING GLOVES

- **Fight the good fight of faith**

P aul told Timothy to fight the good fight of faith. If you want to live your best life now, you must be willing to fight the good fight of faith.

2 Timothy 4:7 (AMP) *I have fought the good (worthy, honorable, and noble) fight, I have finished the race, I have kept (firmly held) the faith.*

- **If you want to live your best life now, you must never accept defeat.**
  To live in victory, you must never accept defeat.

Jack Dempsey, former world heavyweight boxing champion said, *A champion is one who gets up when he can't.* Too many Christians come under attack and give up in the heat of battle. All they want to do is sit down, roll over and play dead. They think if I don't do anything for the Kingdom, maybe the devil won't notice me and will leave me alone. **WRONG thinking again!** When you lay down and play dead, you are giving the devil a green light to kick you around the soccer field of life like a ball and you will live a life of defeat.

- **How do you know when defeat has set in?**
  When you are living in defeat, your progress is stopped in its tracks.

When you are living in defeat you have allowed the devil to put you in neutral and you are simply spinning your wheels and going nowhere. When you are living in defeat you are no longer able to make a difference in the Kingdom of God. When you are living in defeat your prayer life stops. When you are living in defeat your devotional life stops.

When you are living in defeat your commitment and service to God receives a serious blow. Some folks who are sitting in pews haven't done anything for the Kingdom for far too long. God wants to change that! God wants to bring you out of that place of unfruitfulness into a land flowing with milk and honey.

Some followers of Christ have all kinds of reasons for not doing anything for God. Some blame the lack of time, or state, "I am too busy." Others say they are tired and burnt out. Some say "I did it for years now let someone else do it." Many times we look for any excuse not to give God our best. Sometimes we make serving God sound like we are doing time in prison. There is something wrong with that picture.

- Don't live a life of defeat; get up and do something.
  If you want to live your best life now, you must be willing to take action. You must be willing to do something for God. You must be willing to start somewhere, start where you are now. Someone once said: *Some men have thousands of reasons why they cannot do what they want to, when all they need is one reason why they can.* I want to tell you a story about a high school football team called *Put Johnson In The Game*[4]. The story is about a high school football player named Johnson.

Put Johnson In The Game!
It was the middle of a high school football game, emotions were high and the home team was losing badly. They just couldn't seem to get any positive momentum going whatsoever. Nothing seemed to be working in their favor. One irate fan yells at the coaches on the sideline, *"Put Johnson in, put Johnson in, put*

---

4 *Unknown author*

Johnson in the game!" One of the coaches on the sideline yells back, *"Johnson is already in the game!"* The fan yells back again, *"Take Johnson out, take Johnson out, take Johnson out!"* The moral of the story is, if what you are doing in life is not working, do something different. Don't just sit there twiddling your thumbs doing nothing, start somewhere, don't be afraid to try something different.

> *Some men have thousands of reasons why they cannot do what they want to, when all they need is one reason why they can.*

In 2 Kings Chapter Seven there is a story about the city of Samaria under siege. The people had no food, most of the animals had been eaten and the people in the city were starving to death. Four lepers lay at the gate discussing their options.

1. We can go into the city and die.
2. We can stay here and die.
3. We can go over to the Arameans; if they spare us we live.
4. If they kill us we die.

The key thing to learn is they decided to do something.
Many times God will reward a person with the right heart who is willing to do something even when they can't see how all the pieces fit. This is the action you should take instead of just sitting there twiddling your thumbs doing nothing.

God rewards faith that is put into action.
Because the four lepers were willing to do something, three blessings presented themselves.

1. They found the enemy had left
2. They found food
3. They found treasure

All these blessings happened because they took a risk and were willing to do something. *If you're not living on the edge, you're taking up too much space,* (Otis Broadwater). Dare to take a step out of the shadows of fearfulness and uncertainty; start from where you are and do something. When Peter got out of the boat and walked on water, we don't hear about a mad rush behind him of others jumping in. Peter was willing to take a risk, therefore he took action. If you want to live your best life now, you must get up off your hind quarters and do something.

> *If you want to live your best life now, you must get up off your hind quarters and do something.*

Chapter Summary

- What are you willing to do to help build God's Kingdom? **Ecclesiastes 9:10a (AMP)** *Whatever your hand finds to do, do it with all your might.*

Erma Bombeck: *When I stand before God at the end of my life, I would hope that I would not have a single bit of talent left and could say, "I used everything you gave me."*

Chapter Thirteen

FIGHT FOR WHAT YOU BELIEVE

1 Timothy 6:12 (KJV) *Fight the good fight of faith, lay hold on eternal life, whereunto thou art also called, and hast professed a good profession before many witnesses.*

- **If you want to live your best life now, you must let God fight your battles.**

  2 Chronicles 20:9 (NCV) *If trouble comes upon us, or war, punishment, sickness, or hunger, we will stand before you and before this Temple where you have chosen to be worshiped. We will cry out to you when we are in trouble. Then you will hear and save us.*

Exodus 14:14 (NLT) *The Lord himself will fight for you. You won't have to lift a finger in your defense!"*

Throughout Scripture again and again the Bible says God will defend us.

But the devil keeps telling you, you must defend yourself. It's time to stop believing the devil's lies and start believing what God's Word says. God is a just God and He will repay the exact compensation owed to you. He will settle and solve the cases of His people.

Hebrews 10:30 (NCV) *We know that God said, "I will punish those who do wrong; I will repay them."*

And He also said, *"The Lord will judge his people."* Are you dealing with an unresolved case from your past that is stealing your peace and needs resolution? Are you waiting for your day of justice and repayment? God promises in His Word that He is your vindicator. He is your defender. He will settle your case and repay everything the enemy has stolen. But in order to allow Jesus to settle your debts, you have to forgive others in the same way Jesus forgave you when you were guilty of sin. You have to

107

release those who have wronged you from what you think they owe you. That's true forgiveness.

True forgiveness is making a conscious decision to let others go free even if they don't deserve it. When you make a decision to free others, you free yourself. When you live a life of forgiveness, you show to others that you have put your trust and faith in God to be your defender. God will honor your faith in Him and move on your behalf every single time.

- **If you want to live your best life now, you must know God will deliver you.**
  One thing I want you to know and ingrain deeply as possible in your mind and heart is that no matter how tight the chains that Satan tries to imprison you with are; your God will deliver you!

Psalm 107:20 (KJV) *He sent his word, and healed them, and delivered them from their destructions.*

Psalm 91:15 (MSG) *Call me and I'll answer, be at your side in bad times; I'll rescue you, then throw you a party.*

II Cor. 1:10 (MSG) *And he did it, rescued us from certain doom. And he'll do it again, rescuing us as many times as we need rescuing.*

- **If you want to live your best life now, you must know victory belongs to you.**
  Victory belongs to you; it is your birth right as a child of God.

Psalm 44:7-8 (NIV) *But you give us victory over our enemies, you put our adversaries to shame. (v8) In God we make our boast all day long, and we will praise your name forever.*

God has commanded victory to be yours!

And when God commands something, it's going to happen!

When God commanded light to come, light came at 186,000 miles per second – and light still obeys God's command. God has commanded that we live in victory.

That means no matter what you're going through, no matter how dark it may look in your life right now, be encouraged because that darkness has to give way to the light. Defeat has to give way to victory! But in order to open the door to victory, we must continually do what the psalmist did and constantly praise the Lord's name. Don't go around talking about your problems; instead, go around talking about your God and His solutions. Don't go around speaking words of defeat and failure; speak words of faith, hope and victory. Quit worrying about what could go wrong. But rather, start praising God for what has gone right. Praise and thank God right in the midst of trouble, then stand back and watch God work.

> *True forgiveness is making a conscious decision to let others go free even if they don't deserve it. When you make a decision to free others, you free yourself.*

- **Pursue Your Victory - Don't Dwell on The Past**
  It's time like never before to be aggressive and energetic when it comes to letting go of the past and pressing forward to the abundant life God has for you. It's time to develop a warrior mentality and proactively pursue the happiness, health, strength and peace God has promised you in His Word.

God told Joshua to cross over the Jordan and go in and possess the Promised Land. To possess implies action. It means to drive out the previous tenants.

Jesus said in **Matthew 11:12,** *The kingdom of heaven suffers violence, but the violent take it by force.*

> *Don't go around talking about your problems; instead, go around talking about your God and His solutions.*

God told the children of Israel to go in and take by force the land He had given them. **Deuteronomy 7:1-2 (NIV)** *When the LORD your God brings you into the land you are entering to possess and drives out before you many nations--the Hittites, Girgashites, Amorites, Canaanites, Perizzites, Hivites and Jebusites, seven nations larger and stronger than you—v2 and when the LORD your God has delivered them over to you and you have defeated them, then you must destroy them totally. Make no treaty with them, and show them no mercy.*

Take a close look at what God told the children of Israel to do, (1) destroy them totally (2) make no treaty with them and

(3) show them no mercy. This is exactly the way God wants us to treat the devils and demons which try to steal God's blessings from us.

Always remember when you go to war against the devil you are not alone, Jesus is with you.

Deut. 28:7 (NCV) *The LORD will help you defeat the enemies that come to fight you. They will attack you from one direction, but they will run from you in seven directions.*

It's time to stop dwelling on past mistakes and failures, and purpose in your heart to never look back! As you set your focus on the Word of God and His promises, you'll discover His abundance of joy, peace and prosperity in every area of your life.

Philippians 3:13-14 (KJV) *Brethren, I count not myself to have apprehended: but this one thing I do, forgetting those things which are behind, and reaching forth unto those things which are before, [14] I press toward the mark for the prize of the high calling of God in Christ Jesus.*

- **If you want to live your best life now, you must learn how to stand strong during times of adversity.**
  Ephesians 6:13 (TLB) *So use every piece of God's armor to resist the enemy whenever he attacks, and when it is all over, you will still be standing up.*

We all face challenges and difficult times in life. Sometimes things get so dark that we can barely see where to place our next step. I often say to the church that "Sometimes things get darker than the darkest dark." Someone from the congregation will cry out, "How dark?" Then I say, "Darker than a thousand midnights in a black lagoon. So dark that someone has to pipe sunlight down, then someone comes and steals the pipe. That's pretty dark!"

In Psalms 23 David said, *although I find myself walking through the valley of the shadow of death I will fear no evil because I know my God is with me.*

In **Psalms 18:28 KJV** David further said, *my God will enlighten my darkness.*

If God did it for David, He will do it for you and for me. Where do the storms of life come from? Does God send them? No! The storms of life come from the wicked one, the devil. The devil is the one who wants to destroy our marriages, our families, our finances and our very lives if we allow him to have his way.

John 10:10 (KJV) *The thief cometh not, but for to steal, and to kill, and to destroy: I am come that they might have life, and that they might have it more abundantly.*

Every test and trial the devil brings our way is an opportunity to allow God's Word to come alive in your life and see you through to victory. You can't run from everything that's hard in your life because God did not deliver you immediately. God uses these challenges to stretch you and enlarge your faith.

The Apostle James said; *think it not strange when fiery test and trials come to test you.* God uses these challenges for us to seek Him, and grow deeper in our relationship with Him. Remaining faithful during times of adversity is how we grow spiritually.

Make up your mind to serve God no matter what comes against you, and God will honor you. Remember, God never wastes a hurt or any painful experience we go through. Somehow God causes all things to work together for our good **(Romans 8:28).** Simply remain faithful and fight the good fight of faith. In due season, in God's appointed time, He will deliver you, and promote you to new levels of victory and success in Him if you don't give up.

I Peter 4:12 (MSG) *Friends, when life gets really difficult, don't jump to the conclusion that God isn't on the job.*

- **If you want to live your best life now, you must be Prepared to Overcome Opposition**.
  James 1:2-4 (TLB) *Dear brothers, is your life full of difficulties and temptations? Then be happy, ³for when the way is rough, your patience has a chance to grow. ⁴So let it grow, and don't try to squirm out of your problems. For when your patience is finally in full bloom, then you will be ready for anything, strong in character, full and complete.*

Adversity visits us all from time to time, and in many different ways. Adversity can come disguised as marriage problems, sickness, financial calamity, hardships from personal attacks, or difficulty in the workplace.

Adversity is no respecter of persons. All of us will face this menace of darkness one day. The question is not will it happen, but rather how we will respond.

There is a Scripture in the Word of God that reveals, *If thou faint in the day of adversity thy strength is small* (Proverbs 24:10). In this context, fainting doesn't mean to literally lose consciousness; rather it means to withdraw, let go, or to show signs of weakness.

> *Every test and trial the devil brings our way is an opportunity to allow God's Word to come alive in your life and see you through to victory.*

When adversity hits, most people have a tendency to look for a way out, they simply want to escape. The Lord is very specific in this verse, He makes it clear that withdrawing from adversity is not the way to go. He also makes it clear that if we back off during times of trouble, it means we lack spiritual strength and show weakness. When you are faced with opposition in life, know God will open a door in the spirit realm for you to pass through safely.

I Cor. 16:9 (MSG) *A huge door of opportunity for good work has opened up here.* (There is also mushrooming opposition)

God is always giving us opportunities to move forward in life. It is

God's desire to see you grow and reach your full potential. Anytime you take a step forward, the enemy will try to bring opposition and adversity against you to throw you off track and stop you. In I Cor. 16:9 Paul realized when God opened for him a wide door of opportunity, it brought with it many new challenges and spiritual attacks.

> *We can use the storms of life to rise to greater heights. Achieve greater challenges that will lead us to new adventures as we learn how to use them to our advantage.*

The devil is not going to sit idly by doing nothing while God is blessing your socks off! God promises through Him you can overcome any opposition the enemy brings your way.

2 Corinthians 2:14 (KJV) *Now thanks be unto God, which always causeth us to triumph in Christ.*

Luke 10:19 (KJV) *Behold, I give unto you power to tread on serpents and scorpions, and over all the power of the enemy: and nothing shall by any means hurt you.*

When you step out in faith, and opposition comes, stand your ground and keep doing what you know is right. Paul told Timothy to fight the good fight of faith.

Keep on praying, keep on reading your Bible, keep on going to church, keep on walking in love, and keep on walking in forgiveness. Keep your heart tender and speak words of hope and victory over your life and the lives of others. When the enemy sees you are more determined than he is, he'll back down and back off, and you'll move forward to new levels of victory and happiness in God like never before.

- **Call on God in times of trouble**
  Psalm 50:15 (GW) *Call on me in times of trouble. I will rescue you, and you will honor me.*

Psalm 91:5-7 (TEV) *You need not fear any dangers at night or sudden attacks during the day* ⁶ *or the plagues that strike in the dark or the evils that kill in daylight.* ⁷ *A thousand may fall dead beside you, ten thousand all around you, but you will not be harmed.*

Psalm 91:14-15 (KJV) *Because he hath set his love upon me, therefore will I deliver him: I will set him on high, because he hath known my name.* ¹⁵ *He shall call upon me, and I will answer him: I will be with him in trouble; I will deliver him, and honour him.*

When trouble comes, ask God what to do.

I Samuel 30:7-8 (TLB) *Then he said to Abiathar the priest, "Bring the oracle!" So Abiathar brought it. David asked the Lord, "Shall I chase them? Will I catch them?" And the Lord told him, "Yes, go after them; you will recover everything that was taken from you!"*

- **Know God will keep you during times of trouble.**
  Isaiah 26:3, 4 *You keep him in perfect peace whose mind is stayed on you, because he trusts in you. Trust in the LORD forever, for the LORD GOD is an everlasting rock.*

- **If you are going to live your best life now, you must become an eagle warrior.**
  Eagles don't run from the storms of life, eagles love the storm. When clouds gather, eagles get excited. The eagle uses the

storm's wind to lift it higher. Once it finds the wind of the storm, the eagle uses the raging storm to lift him above the clouds. This gives the eagle an opportunity to glide and rest its wings. In the meantime, all the other birds hide in the leaves and branches of the trees scared to death with their knees shaking. We can use the storms of life to rise to greater heights. Achieve greater challenges that will lead us to new adventures as we learn how to use them to our advantage.

- **If you want to live your best life now, you must fight to break Free From Family Curses.**
  Jeremiah 31:29 (NRSV) *In those days they shall no longer say: "The parents have eaten sour grapes, and the children's teeth are set on edge."*

In order to get set free and stay free, you must admit you have a problem and the thread of it has been passed down from generation to generation. That sounds simple, but we live in a day and age of denial. No matter what has happened to us in our lives, each of us are responsible for the choices and decisions we make. If you want to live your best life now you must recognize the curse, disown it and break free from it in the name of Jesus. God wants you to be the one to apply your faith and turn a new page in your family's history. He wants you to break any generational curses that may be standing between you and your desire to live your best life now.

Chapter Summary

- **Dare to believe you have power with God**
  The Bible says out of the mouths of two or three witnesses let every word be established. The following Scriptures shine light on the fact that as followers of Christ we have power with God.

Acts 1:8 (KJV) *But ye shall receive power, after that the Holy Ghost is come upon you: and ye shall be witnesses unto me both in Jerusalem, and in all Judaea, and in Samaria, and unto the uttermost part of the earth.*

Luke 10:19 (NLT) *And I have given you authority over all the power of the enemy, and you can walk among snakes and scorpions and crush them. Nothing will injure you.*

Ephesians 3:20 (KJV) *Now unto him that is able to do exceeding abundantly above all that we ask or think, according to the power that worketh in us.*

Philippians 4:13 (KJV) *I can do all things through Christ which strengtheneth me.*

2 Corinthians 2:14 (KJV) *Now thanks be unto God, which always causeth us to triumph in Christ.*

Chapter Fourteen

TAKE
ADVANTAGE OF
OPPORTUNITIES

If you want to live your best life now, you must take advantage of opportunities God sends your way.

John 7:6 (AMP) *Whereupon Jesus said to them, My time (opportunity) has not come yet; but any time is suitable for you and your opportunity is ready any time [is always here].*

Proverbs 10:5 (TLB) *A wise youth makes hay while the sun shines, but what a shame to see a lad who sleeps away his hour of opportunity.*

1 Corinthians 16:9a (AMP) *For a wide door of opportunity for effectual [service] has opened to me [there, a great and promising one].*

We all love to hear the word 'opportunity' roll off our lips, knock on our door, or enter our thoughts. New opportunities for a better life are something most people are willing to receive with open arms.

> *There is something about the word opportunity that inspires hope and stirs new thoughts and possibilities for a more fulfilling life.*

There is something about the word opportunity that inspires hope and stirs new thoughts and possibilities for a more fulfilling life. How many of you have heard it said that opportunity only knocks once? That's true in some cases, but in my observation, opportunity not only knocks once, but twice and sometimes even for a third time. Opportunity is like a sales person who knocks on your door again and again or calls you on the phone when you're busy eating dinner and you don't want to be bothered. You don't want to stop and open the door because you're enjoying your food, and you wish this uninvited guest would simply disappear or go away. We don't want to stop because we have heard sales pitches again and again and we aren't interested in hearing another. Many times good opportunities aren't immediately seen. Sometimes they drop by as unexpected guests at the most unexpected and inopportune times.

When opportunity presents itself, your attitude may determine whether or not you live your best life now or miss out on what could be. Opportunity can be a single event that crosses your path and enlightens you, changes your direction in life and points you in a new direction. Many times opportunity is simply the voice of the Holy Spirit trying to get through the busyness of everyday life to bless you. Unfortunately, because of our busy lifestyles and insensitivity to God's voice, we miss out on many wonderful opportunities to receive God's best.

Chapter Summary

Thomas Edison said: *Opportunity is missed by most people because it is dressed in overalls and looks like work.*

Chapter Fifteen

BE WILLING TO MAKE SACRIFICES

If you want to live your best life now, you must be willing to make sacrifices.

Romans 12:1 (KJV) *I beseech you therefore, brethren, by the mercies of God, that ye present your bodies a living sacrifice, holy, acceptable unto God, which is your reasonable service.*

Romans 12:1 (NIV) *Therefore, I urge you, brothers, in view of God's mercy, to offer your bodies as living sacrifices, holy and pleasing to God--this is your spiritual act of worship.*

The act of personal surrender can be called many things: consecration, making Jesus Lord, taking up your cross, dying to self, or yielding to the Spirit.

These are just a few ways of saying I give myself completely to God. I don't think it's so important what you call it; what matters most is that you do it. The principle of the living sacrifice is found throughout the Scriptures. The sacrifice offering is found in the tabernacles of Moses, David, and Solomon. All of these temples in the Old Testament were made with mortar and stone. But in the New Testament God is building a temple of flesh.

The Bible says we are living stones that make up a spiritual building called the Church. Just as God required a living sacrifice under the old covenant, He requires nothing less of us today. God wants us to give Him ourselves as a living sacrifice. Giving a sacrifice offering involves making sacrifices. When we give a sacrificial offering to God, He wants us to give Him the things we love most in life. God wants us to give Him the things that are stopping us from giving Him our best.

In 2 Samuel Chapter 24, David said he would not give an offering unto God which did not cost him something. In other words, David was saying our offerings unto God must involve sacrifice.

> *The act of personal surrender can be called many things: consecration, making Jesus Lord, taking up your cross, dying to self, or yielding to the Spirit.*

2 Samuel 24:20-25 (KJV) *And Araunah looked, and saw the king and his servants coming on toward him: and Araunah went out, and bowed himself before the king on his face upon the ground. [21] And Araunah said, Wherefore is my lord the king come to his servant? And David said, To buy the threshingfloor of thee, to build an altar unto the LORD, that the plague may be stayed from the people. [22] And Araunah said unto David, Let my lord the king take and offer up what seemeth good unto him: behold, here be oxen for burnt sacrifice, and threshing instruments and other instruments of the oxen for wood. [23] All these things did Araunah, as a king, give unto the king. And Araunah said unto the king, The LORD thy God accept thee. [24] And the king said unto Araunah, Nay; but I will surely buy it of thee at a price: neither will I offer burnt offerings unto the LORD my God of that which doth cost me nothing. So David bought the threshingfloor and the oxen for fifty shekels of silver. [25] And David built there an altar unto the LORD, and offered burnt offerings and peace offerings. So the LORD was intreated for the land, and the plague was stayed from Israel.*

When you are willing to make sacrifices that others will not, it will take you to places that others can only dream about. Sacrifice is like a bill collector that knocks on your door again and again asking to be paid. The million dollar question is; will you pay him or send him away? The more you want to be used by God, the more you must be willing to give up the things you love most in life.

Martin Luther King, Jr. said, *If a man hasn't discovered something worth dying for, he isn't fit to live.*[5] The majority of his adult life he lived a sacrificial life. He was stoned, stabbed, and physically attacked[6]. His house was bombed and his family threatened. He gave his life for the cause of freedom and paid the ultimate sacrifice when he was assassinated. Over 50 years later, our hearts are still stirred by Martin Luther's King's famous *I Have A Dream* speech.

> *When you are willing to make sacrifices that others will not, it will take you to places that others can only dream about.*

- **If you want to live your best life now, you too must be willing to get out of the boat and take a chance!**

Matthew 14:25-29 (CEV) *A little while before morning, Jesus came walking on the water toward his disciples. [26] When they saw him, they thought he was a ghost. They were terrified and started screaming. [27] At once, Jesus said to them, "Don't worry!*

---

5   Quote from Dr. Martin Luther King's speech in Detroit

6   References from the Chicago Tribune and NBC News, New York

I am Jesus. Don't be afraid." [28] Peter replied, "Lord, if it is really you, tell me to come to you on the water." [29] "Come on!" Jesus said. Peter then got out of the boat and started walking on the water toward him.

Say "Yes" to new opportunities and possibilities of living your best life now. In Chapter Fourteen I talked about the importance of taking advantage of opportunities that God sends your way. I want to end this chapter by revisiting the importance of taking advantage of opportunities. The thought of living your best life now brings with it **new and fresh opportunities to change** your life forever. If you allow your heart to be open to God, you will hear His voice and receive the guidance you need to live a winning and victorious Christian life.

> *Taking advantage of new opportunities can be scary, but if you want to live your best life now, you must be willing to take a chance.*

Your actions will determine if you live your best life now or miss out on an opportunity handed to you today on a silver platter. You need to read this book over and over again until you get it deeply engrained within your spirit and soul. The thought you can live your best life now must become a part of who you are, not who you want to be.

Living your best life now will help you find a missing part of yourself that you desperately need to discover. Taking advantage of new opportunities can be scary, but if you want to live your best life now, you must be willing to take a chance. Trust your gut, which is the voice of the Holy Spirit trying to help you make wise choices and lead you down the right path. If you want to receive God's best, sometimes you must be willing to go for it. You also must be willing to take a leap of faith, and be willing to do things you have never done before.

Chapter Summary

The beauty of taking chances is that anything can happen and the sky becomes your limit! You might fail or get embarrassed, but what if you could experience something that is completely mind-blowing that will change your life forever. Dare to step out in faith from where you are now and step back and watch God go to work on your behalf.

Chapter Sixteen

THE
BLESSING OF
GIVING

Luke 6:38 (TLB) *For if you give, you will get! Your gift will return to you in full and overflowing measure, pressed down, shaken together to make room for more, and running over. Whatever measure you use to give—large or small—will be used to measure what is given back to you.*

- **If you want to live your best life now, you must be a giver.**
  Galatians 6:10 (NLT) *Therefore, whenever we have the opportunity, we should do good to everyone—especially to those in the family of faith.*

The Taco Bell Story

My granddaughter Tamara called me one day with an interesting story about giving. She was telling me how she had just got off work and was really hungry and planned to go to Taco Bell to get a burrito. She had envisioned herself eating this burrito before she arrived there. She could taste the delicious flavors bursting in her mouth and smell the aroma before she had it in her hand. She pulled into the drive thru and ordered a burrito. She paid for it, grabbed her bag and was on her way. She could hardly wait to take her first bite. Just when she got to a stoplight and pulled out her burrito, there was a homeless man right there on the side of the road begging. Her first thought was to give him a little money to get something to eat; then the Holy Spirit spoke to her, and told her to give the man her Taco Bell burrito. At first, she thought; "Oh no!" But the Holy Spirit quickly softened her heart and she gave him her burrito. He thanked her, and then she turned around and headed back to Taco Bell to get another burrito. She pulled into the drive thru for a second time and placed her order. The guy taking the order said, "Weren't you just in here a few minutes ago?" She said "Yes" and began to share with him the story of how she had given her burrito to a homeless man begging at a stop light. The man then told her because she was so generous to someone in need, Taco Bell was going to bless her by paying for her food. Well, I guess the saying is true: It's more blessed to give than it is to receive.

Chapter Summary

II Corinthians 9:9 (NLT) *Godly people give generously. Their good deeds will never be forgotten.*

Chapter Seventeen

WALK IN
GOD'S
WISDOM

The importance of walking in God's wisdom

You never will be able to live your best life now without learning how to walk in God's wisdom.

Let's take a look at the seven pillars of wisdom

Proverbs 9:1 (KJV) *Wisdom hath builded her house, she hath hewn out her seven pillars.*

If you want to live your best life now, you must learn how to operate in the full wisdom of God. Out of all the things I have talked about in living your best life over the last sixteen chapters, learning how to walk in God's wisdom is perhaps the crowning jewel of them all. God's wisdom in a nutshell is basically a wise and prudent application of the knowledge God has blessed us with. In this chapter, we will take a look at seven building blocks that can become pillars of strength in your life. Applying these principles to your life will help you stand tall and firm against the wiles of the devil and the storms of life that come your way.

The wisdom of God is like a special protective garment that has the ability to adjust in all types of weather.

The wisdom of God is like a special protective garment that has the ability to adjust in all types of weather. There are at least seven pieces to the full picture of God's wisdom. Understanding these seven pillars will help you paint a word picture and give you a mental overview of what God's wisdom looks like, and how you can apply it to your everyday life.

1. **The first pillar is plain old everyday Common Sense Wisdom**

   The Hebrew word for common sense is **Sekel**. The word **Sekel** means *intelligence; common sense, and practical insight into the affairs of everyday life.*

   Psalm 119:66 (MSG) *Train me in good common sense; I'm thoroughly committed to living your way.*

   - **If you want to live your best life now, you are going to need a barrel full of plain old everyday common sense.** **Proverbs 7:4 (CEV)** *Let wisdom be your sister and make common sense your closest friend.*

     Warren Buffet said: '*A wise man will do in the beginning what the fool will do in the end.*'

     David prayed a prayer that God would give him Sekel, which is wisdom for common sense.

     Psalm 119:169 (TLB) says: *O Lord, listen to my prayers; give me the common sense you promised.*

2. **The second pillar of wisdom that you will need to live your best life now is Holy Character**

   1 Peter 1:15-16 (CEV) *Always live as God's holy people should, because God is the one who chose you, and he is holy. [16] That's why the Scriptures say, "I am the holy God, and you must be holy too."*

   1 Peter 2:5 (KJV) *Ye also, as lively stones, are built up a spiritual house, an holy priesthood, to offer up spiritual sacrifices, acceptable to God by Jesus Christ.*

   If you want to live your best life now, holy character

must be a part of who you are, not who you seek to be but who you are now.

What is holy character? Wisdom for holy character helps us choose the good and refuse the evil in every area of life. Wisdom for holy character will help you determine where you should go and where you should not go. It will help you develop a lifestyle which pleases God and gives Him honor. Holy character will help you avoid dishonor and shame.

Let's take a look at the words of Solomon about Holy Character.

Proverbs 1:1-3 (NCV) *These are the wise words of Solomon son of David, king of Israel. ²They teach wisdom and self-control; they will help you understand wise words. 3They will teach you how to be wise and self-controlled and will teach you to do what is honest and fair and right.*

Wisdom for holy character makes for a happier life.

Proverbs 11:5-6 MSG) *Moral character makes for smooth traveling; an evil life is a hard life. 6Good character is the best insurance; crooks get trapped in their sinful lust.*

Wisdom for holy character will help you live your best life now.

3. **God's Wisdom for finances is needed if you want to prosper and succeed in life**
Joshua 1:8 (KJV) *This book of the law shall not depart out of thy mouth; but thou shalt meditate therein day and night, that thou mayest observe to do according to all that is written therein: for then thou shalt make thy way prosperous, and then thou shalt have good success.*

The Hebrew word for success in Joshua 1:8 is **Sakal**.

Sakal is God's wisdom for financial success and victory.

Some people think because they are Christians and love Jesus, their finances will fall in line with God's Word and money will come their way like a runaway train on a steep hill. But nothing could be further from the truth! Just because you have Jesus in you doesn't mean you are filled to the brim with wisdom for finances. You may not realize that you can have wisdom in one area but lack in another.

Ecclesiastes 9:14-15 (NKJV) *There was a little city with few men in it; and a great king came against it, besieged it, and built great snares around it. [15] Now there was found in it a poor wise man, and he by his wisdom delivered the city. Yet no one remembered that same poor man.*

Just because you are saved and operating in wisdom in some areas does not mean you have wisdom for finances. When it comes to money, why do you think some Christians are successful and others are not? One thing that seems obvious to me is that some Christians are making right choices while others are making wrong choices.

Some have tapped into the wisdom of **Sakal** for finances and it's working for them and others have not. The biggest single key I know that can destroy the spirit of poverty and lack is the wisdom of God for finances. If you want to become a person empowered with spiritual wisdom to overcome poverty and lack in your life, the truths found on these pages will lead you into financial freedom. Jesus said you shall know the truth and the truth will set you free.

The wisdom of **Sakal** will help you find the financial success and victory you have been looking for. **Sir Frances Bacon said:** *Knowledge is power.*

Romans 10:17 (KJV) the Bible says: *So then faith cometh by hearing, and hearing by the word of God.*

Hosea said, *God's people are destroyed for a lack of knowledge.*

Don't ever let the enemy bombard your mind with false thoughts which make you believe it's not God's will for the preacher to instruct you in the area of finances…because it is! God wants to equip you with the information you need to succeed financially.

> *If you want to live your best life now, holy character must be a part of who you are, not who you seek to be but who you are now.*

4. **If you want to live your best life now, you will need God's wisdom for new strategies**
   Proverbs 8:12 (KJV) *I wisdom dwell with prudence, and find out knowledge of witty inventions.*

The Hebrew word used here for wisdom is **Chakam.**

Chakam is a skillful use of wisdom to create, develop, and see new ideals and approaches to problems in everything we desire to accomplish.

Exodus 31:3-4 (KJV) *And I have filled him with the spirit of God, in wisdom, and in understanding, and in knowledge, and in all manner of workmanship, [4] To devise cunning works, to work in gold, and in silver, and in brass.*

Wisdom for new ideals and strategies is a God-given ability.

Chakam is the ability to devise wise, solid and fruitful plans to expand the Kingdom of God, bless the Church and our personal lives. It is a gift from God.

Wisdom for new strategies is a God-inspired ability to be creative and to think outside the box. Men and women with this gifting remind me of an old TV series I used to watch called the *A-Team*. The *A-Team* were problem solvers, they demonstrated innovative ways to bring a plan together and make it work. Hannibal, the brains behind the *A Team*, had a habit of saying he loves it when a plan comes together. God loves it also. Wisdom for new strategies is the ability to see how the pieces of an unsolved problem or challenge fits together before others see it.

5. **If you want to live your best life now, you must be skillful in the use of God's wisdom**
   Proverbs 15:2 (KJV) *The tongue of the wise useth knowledge aright: but the mouth of fools poureth out foolishness.*

The Hebrew word used here for wise is **Chok-math** which means to be wise (in mind, word or acts). **Chok-math** comes from the root word **Chakam** which means skillful. The Strong's Dictionary defines **Chok-math** as a skillful, artful, and cunning use of wisdom. To operate in **Chok-math** means to skillfully apply knowledge to the various circumstances life brings your way. God is looking for men and women who are skilled in the use of wisdom.

2 Chronicles 2:7 (KJV) *Send me now therefore a man cunning to work in gold, and in silver, and in brass, and in* *iron, and in purple, and crimson, and blue, and that can skill to grave with the cunning men that are with me in Judah and in Jerusalem, whom David my father did provide.*

To be skillful in the use of wisdom, you must know when to use a hammer and when to use a scalpel. It takes the wisdom of **Chok-math** to skillfully use God's Word. Don't be like a bull in a china shop.

Hebrews 4:12 (KJV) *For the word of God is quick, and powerful, and sharper than any two edged sword, piercing even to the dividing asunder of soul and spirit, and of the joints and marrow, and is a discerner of the thoughts and intents of the heart.*

6. Wisdom for spiritual insight

I Chron. 12:32a (KJV) *And of the children of Issachar, which were men that had understanding of the times, to know what Israel ought to do.*

Jesus was rich in spiritual insight
John 4:13-14 (KJV) *Jesus answered and said unto her, Whosoever drinketh of this water shall thirst again: ¹⁴ But whosoever drinketh of the water that I shall give him shall never thirst; but the water that I shall give him shall be in him a well of water springing up into everlasting life.*

If you want to live your best life now and have the bright future promised in God's Word, you must make General Christian wisdom a regular part of your diet.

Wisdom for spiritual insight is a God-given ability to see in three different time zones, the past, the present, and the future.

- **Wisdom to see the past**
- **Wisdom to see the present**
- **Wisdom to see your next move in life**

How many of you play chess? Wisdom for spiritual insight is like playing a chess game; you must know what your next best move is. Wisdom for spiritual insight is the ability to glean spiritual insight and wisdom from past mistakes made by yourself or others, learn from where you are now, and have insight about the future. Wisdom for spiritual insight is a God-given ability to envision or see the outcome of what you are about to do before you do it. God's wisdom for spiritual insight will help you walk in a greater measure of God's peace because you will not have to undo as many things because you did not foresee the outcome. God's wisdom for spiritual insight will help you avoid tearing down bridges that you would later have to come back and build again. The wisdom of spiritual insight helps you think things through before you do them. Wisdom for spiritual insight reduces the need for many apologies of avoidable mistakes. Wisdom for spiritual insight will reduce the need for many Holy Spirit wood shed experiences. Turn to yourself and say *I know that's right!* The wisdom of spiritual insight will help you hit the bull's eye more often, or at least hit the target or the wall where it is hanging.

7. General Christian Wisdom

General Christian wisdom is a wisdom that is available to all believers.

James 1:5 (KJV) *If any of you lack wisdom, let him ask of God, that giveth to all men liberally, and upbraideth not; and it shall be given him.*

General Christian wisdom is a mixture of all the different types of wisdom you find in Scripture. The seven pillars of wisdom support our spiritual houses.

Proverbs 9:1-2 (NKJV) *Wisdom has built her house, She has hewn out her seven pillars; ² She has slaughtered her meat, She has mixed her wine, She has also furnished her table.*

The seven pillars of God's wisdom provide everything you need. To put it simply, **General Christian Wisdom** is a skillful blending or mixing together of all the wines of wisdom in one glass and drinking it. If you want to live your best life now, you must take the mixed drink of General Christian Wisdom and say bottoms up, and drink all of it. The mixing of the wines of wisdom in Proverbs 9:2 is a type and shadow of the wisdom James talks about in James 1:5. If you want to live your best life now and have the bright future promised in God's Word, you must make General Christian wisdom a regular part of your diet.

Proverbs 24:13-14 (TEV) *My child, eat honey; it is good. And just as honey from the comb is sweet on your tongue, 14you may be sure that wisdom is good for the soul. Get wisdom and you have a bright future.*

Chapter Summary

- **If you want to live your best life now, you must learn to love wisdom**
  Proverbs 8:17-19 (MSG) *I love those who love me; those who look for me find me. [18]Wealth and Glory accompany me—also substantial Honor and a Good Name. [19]My benefits are worth more than a big salary, even a very big salary; the returns on me exceed any imaginable bonus.*

As you apply the principles you have learned in this book, prepare for new doors and opportunities all around you. Expect the blessings of God to overcome you and become a part of your life.

We Want to Hear from You!

Each week I close our service by giving those who don't know Jesus an opportunity to make Jesus the Lord of their lives. Are you at peace with God? A void exists in every person's heart that only God can fill. I'm not talking about joining a church or finding religion. I'm talking about finding life, peace, and happiness and starting a relationship with our Almighty God!!

Would you pray with me today? Just say, *Lord Jesus, I repent of my sins, I ask you to come into my heart, I make you my Lord and Savior.* Friend, if you prayed this simple prayer, I believe you have been born again. I encourage you to attend a good Bible based church and make Jesus first place in your life.

Contact Information

Pastor Stephen F. Brown

Abundant Life Faith Fellowship Church

2740 Hyannis Drive

Cincinnati, Ohio 45251

Website www.alff.org

email: thealff@alff.org

Made in the USA
Middletown, DE
14 March 2019